Prisoner of Depression

Memoir of An Unexpected Journey

by

Jared Penn

For my mother,

For she went through this journey

with me always by my side...

3

TABLE OF CONTENTS

Preface

Depression. What is it good for? Absolutely nothing. But can it still exist in our lives? Absolutely. Is it ok to have it? Of course. Can it ruin our lives? Only if you choose to let it. The choice is yours to make, and I strongly urge those suffering from it NOT to let it ruin their lives.

It's not worth it. It's not. Life is too precious to just throw away. I'll say it again. LIFE IS TOO PRECIOUS! This is your one shot at making your life extraordinary. There may be times of struggle, or discomfort, and depression may be a causing factor for some. But it shouldn't ruin everything you have going for yourself.

And as for treating it? Everyone deserves the opportunity to deal with it properly, and to receive any form of help coping with it. Judgement does not exist when it comes to depression. Money does not matter when trying to find access to any form of treatment.

Many people still haven't realized that they're suffering from it, and they need to. Shame should not prevent anyone from recognizing their own problems, or even of others you care about. Why be ashamed, when there are millions of others in this world going through the same thing as you?

I had a goal of consolidating everything into a book or partial autobiography, about the era of my depression. This book would act as my guide through the rest of my life. Every time I read it and use it as a reference to my past experiences, it will motivate me to continue living healthy. I would encourage others to read it, for they may find some of it helpful.

My intention is to share my story, where my chosen readers will know what I went through, and how difficult and heartbreaking it was. Also, I would like those suffering from depression to have the opportunity to be aware of it, hoping that they will one day decide to read my inspirational quotes. No matter how many people read it, I hope it will affect them in some positive way. That's all I can really ask for.

Recently, I made the biggest mistake in my life. I won't say "ever in my entire life" because I still have a whole life ahead of me. No one knows the length of the entirety of their life, so stop acting like there's nothing more to contribute. It's not over, until it's over.

My biggest mistake, so far, and hopefully the last one, was trying to kill myself. I had been through hardship for several years, losing important relationships and values for recognizing my true self. I dealt with depression for many years. I will continue to deal with it, probably for the rest of my life. But it shouldn't end my life. It shouldn't end anyone's life.

We live in a world today where depression is embraced to be recognized and tolerated. Why else do you think we have therapists, medication, and treatment centers? They didn't appear out of thin air for no apparent reason. It's because we have adapted as human beings to realize that depression does exist. It is a problem among many. It is a real thing.

My suicide attempt unfortunately led to further damage. And no, I'm not talking about myself. In fact, it was property damage, unintended and not part of my plan. The good part of it, ironic to say, was that I didn't go through with ending my life. I panicked, and yet something inside of me told me to escape. "Don't do it! Get out! Save yourself!" Those are just a few examples of what I heard inside my head.

The point is, I heard a voice. Something deep in my conscience wanting to save my life. We may not have complete control of how our mind works, but it sometimes knows when to save us from damaging ourselves.

I was glad about my action and decision, but not about the damage it left behind. And for that, I had to suffer the consequences. I was sent away for my action, for my reckless act that I thought would end in a reasonable choice for myself. The choice of ending my life was not the answer and look where it led me.

Those next several months I spent my time in a psychiatric prison, and then in a county jail after my treatment was *complete. My treatment was not complete during my time there, but it sparked the beginning of my journey to live my life again.*

At the start of this journey in prison, I didn't know what the outcome of this dilemma was going to be. How was it going to resolve? The only resolution I focused on was that I was going to continue living. I'm still going to breathe, to laugh, to cry, to eat, to sleep, and ultimately be happy.

During my time away, I met so many interesting people. Many come from different backgrounds, different lifestyles, ones in which I'd never be familiar with ever again. But for some apparent reason, for some necessary meaning to my life, they'll always stay in my memory. These inmates may be lost souls to the outside world, but they will never be lost from my memories.

An imprint of these shared experiences has been placed in my mind, staying permanent for me to reminisce on when the time comes for it. But who knows, it may haunt me in my dreams. Until then, I hope for the best, and that my thoughts do not wander towards the darkness.

Resiliency is the main theme of this book. I became resilient and overcame some of the toughest obstacles. These obstacles should never be permanent, for they are only temporary. There is always a way to get past them, but it all depends on how much effort you put in finding a way to hurdle the many obstacles that can come across our paths during our lives.

After I went through these obstacles, and finally made it back home from my journey away, I was proud of myself. I felt stronger than before, knowing that I had the power to overcome anything that stood in my way. When someone has that feeling of accomplishment, becoming resilient afterwards when they said to themselves, "I can't do it. It's impossible.", they found their courage. Courage can emanate from anyone deep inside themselves, but it takes courage to find courage.

We need to want to better ourselves, even when we think our situation is impossible to get through. But how else do you know unless you try? Saying to yourself, "I did it.", feels very good. It states that you completed something, and it can be very important to your life. Did you feel any sense of resiliency once you accomplished your goal? Was it difficult reaching that goal? Nothing comes easy in life. And that's something we need to prepare ourselves for.

We practice and strive to make ourselves stronger as human beings, as individuals to know what it takes to achieve what we want in life. Whether we know it or not, we have some form of heroism inside of us. But we're being heroes for ourselves, others too, but mostly for us. Be proud of yourself. Be proud of the small things and be prouder of the big things you've achieved in life.

The measurement between small and big depends on you, and only you. Everyone is different. So, I measure my resiliency after my time in prison as very high. I have a lot of it and intend to keep it for the rest of my life. I am my own Superman. I am my own knight in shining armor. I am proud to get through this horrific struggle, in where I saw things I hope to never see ever again. I was once a prisoner of the state, and I eventually gained my freedom. I am still a prisoner of depression, but I have the freedom to cope with it every day and utilize the right tools to remain happy.

So, why a book? Because I wanted to. Because I needed to. This book, I share with you, is an open invitation to join me on my journey. Your RSVP to this invitation is reading my story, one of many inspiring stories shared by those dealing with depression.

If you choose to accept this offer, then I invite you to the past several years of my life, and for the intense journey of being imprisoned for five months. Experience some moments of my time away that will make you think, laugh, cry, and gain some insight of one suffering from depression.

This book is divided into two parts: my experience living in the psychiatric prison that was majority of my time away, and recorded journal entries sharing important dates and events throughout my journey. My story, in which I share with you, is based on true events.

If you do decide to keep reading on, I thank you from the bottom of my heart. I thank you for your time, for your participation, for your dedication. Most of *all, thank you for you. It's people like you, taking a chance of understanding such topics misunderstood by many, that makes a difference.*

Close your eyes for a moment, take a deep breath, open your eyes, and turn the page. This is my story. This is how…I was a prisoner of depression.

Part I

Psychiatric Prison

For the privacy of those mentioned in this next section, some names have been altered.

Tour of My New Home

"My own life was filled with so much love and joy that when depression struck, it was like a prison door slamming shut and I was being placed in an isolation cell. No one else could possibly be feeling what I was. I hated my depression and all of its symptoms." – Susan Schutz

I always thought my life had hit rock bottom for the past few years. But now, I think it has hit its lowest point. I never thought I would end up in a place like this. The reality of it does not lie. In fact, it's scarier than I anticipated. How did I end up here, in this dump? The truth is, my mental illness caused my being here.

The psychiatric prison was both terrifying and helpful. I say "helpful", because this place was meant to help those in need of mental treatment. Although everyone here is a criminal, this facility was considered a hospital as well.

So, what it is like living in a psychiatric prison?

Let me take you on a tour of what I had to live with for almost five months. Use your imagination of my description to the fullest, but don't get used to wanting to visit such a nightmare, like this place.

When it came to finding out what my room would look like, I was worried about whether I'd have roommates. Luckily, I had my own room, or "cell" as it was properly considered here. I was glad and relieved to be by myself.

I didn't have to worry about another dangerous, insane criminal sharing a tiny room with me. There was no requirement of staying up all night not sleeping, wondering if the roommate was going to do something terrible to me. I was alone, and I preferred that for the first time when all I have wanted for these past few years was to be with others.

The bed in my cell was not so terrible. Sleeping and lying in bed felt fine to me, and I had no complaints. The mattress and pillow were thinly cushioned and looked like it was wrapped in duct tape. That didn't matter, because the sheets and blankets were nicer and suited for sleeping peacefully in the cold dungeon I lived in.

A wooden desk, lacquered and clean without a scratch, was the nicest piece of furniture in my cell. A cushioned stool, which swung out when used, was bolted under the desk. The sound of slow, hissing air would seep out of the seat cushion every time I sat on it. I didn't put much on the desk because I used it mainly for writing.

It served as a table for some of my personal belongings when I wasn't using it for writing. A bottle of lotion for dry skin, the novel I was currently reading, important documents pertaining to my case, and my notebook. I preferred to call it my little office, even if the rest of the cell was my bedroom and bathroom. It was my tiny studio apartment, where the cost of rent is time taken away from my life.

The main area of the ward was wide open with space, and small sections in which to congregate. A dining area for meals was located on one side, consisting of several wooden tables with four seats per table. During these meals, everyone had an assigned seat and table, keeping it consistent with who sat where, without any problems. My table was pretty good, except for one patient who sat across from me, always begging, and hassling me for my food.

There was even one time, on my first day in the ward, where I sat in a different seat that was already assigned to someone else. He confronted me about it, very annoyed, but not pursuing any further arguing or physical interaction. He simply said it was fine because I was new.

A minor warning was all I received, probably because of the type of person I am, which is non-confrontational, and due to how much respect I received from everyone else. Otherwise, I enjoyed the time at my table. It was always quiet, for everyone was shoveling food into their hungry mouths.

The center of the ward was the lounge area. Several rows of cushioned chairs and couches were placed in front of a large, flat screen TV mounted high on the wall for everyone to view. The television was new, consisting of 700 channels, half of which we didn't even get because of the restricted and cheap cable plan. But we had a lot of the usual channels many Americans watch all over the country.

The morning news would be on for the first few hours as we woke up at 6:30 to start the day. The afternoons and evenings were mainly for movies, and at times several TV shows the patients enjoyed watching regularly.

During the weekends, it was all about sports. Football and basketball, both college and professional. The one day where everyone would bond and share their knowledge and love of sports, conversing about stats and players, as if we were actual sports analysts.

On the other side of the ward was the shower and laundry area. Before this area, there is a nurse's station, where medication is given to the patients three times a day: morning, afternoon, and evening. Beyond the nurse's station were two payphones used to contact friends and family.

Next, a large metal barrier to block the view of three individual shower stalls. Each shower stall had a curtain for privacy, although it was half clear to keep watch of anyone doing anything harmful to themselves. A small shower head, powered by a push of a button, released about 15 seconds of water at a time.

Most of the time, the water was ice cold. Depending on how early you showered during shower hours, you have a chance of showering in scorching hot water. There was no median when it came to water temperature here, and warm water did not exist. Not at all.

The guards throughout the facility, or "medical security officers" as what they're properly called, are everywhere. At every entrance to a new hallway and classroom, scattered throughout the hallways in the medical clinics and visiting rooms, they're always there. Every ward is always assigned five officers to watch the patients, making sure violence doesn't occur. I guess that's where the "security" part of their job title comes into place.

As for "medical", not an ounce of medical knowledge within them. Although this facility is considered a mental prison, the officers are not equipped and trained for any mental or medical emergencies. All they know is how to watch patients, lounge in chairs, and sleep on the job.

Both men and women officers share the same minimal job responsibilities. Paperwork is completed daily by them, or should I say, checking off names to see if you've eaten, taken medication, and showered. Nothing difficult or challenging. But overall, the compensation must be decent to consider this their full-time line of work.

The officers in my unit, Unit 6, are very nice, if you behave and cooperate with them. Sometimes they'll offer snacks they sneak in that are usually not available or allowed to patients. Conversing with them always occurs. We'd joke around, talk about our personal lives, maybe sports and news. Creating these relationships and getting to know each other well can make life easier here. With these factors of a guard-to-prisoner relationship, I'd call it "babysitting the criminally insane".

People Are Strange, When You're A Stranger

"While there is a lower class, I am in it, while there is a criminal element, I am of it, and while there is a soul in prison, I am not free." – Eugene V. Debs

During my time here so far, everything has been good. Though sometimes, I feel uncomfortable and ashamed. For someone that has never gotten into serious trouble before, this is a first. Everyone here is perceived as a failure. Others are viewed as nothing but trouble.

But I believe there is some good inside of us, no matter what is troubling our lives. Some people here just need to work harder to find it. Through motivation and determination, hope is achievable.

I feel that some patients here, from what I've seen, choose not to get better. It's almost as if they purposely sabotage themselves, because it is a comfort for them. Their human nature speaks to them in which sabotage is their ultimate destiny. A goal that's reachable and satisfying when they grasp it.

It boggles me as to why they do it. Maybe they gave up, hopeless, to the fact that nothing will work for them. You should never give up on hope. If you believe in it, hope will find a way to reach you.

While I am here, at this facility, I am labeled like everyone else...worthless. I know that I am worth a lot in terms of value. My values have been keeping me alive all this time. These values make me who I am. The characteristics I possess and express determine someone else's first impression of me.

On the outside, I may look like everyone else. ID bracelet on the wrist, a combination of prison clothes, the grisly image of grown out top and facial hair. More importantly, the tension in the shoulders and the anger behind the eyes.

But in my circumstance, my internal traits and qualities show that I am a very educated, successful citizen in society. I have worked too hard to not let all that go. And it shows. It shows.

As I spend my time here, I get to know fellow inmates. Some of them I pass by, I'll give a quick "Hey." or "What's up?". Maybe a fist bump if they're deserving of it. Most of the guys I have gotten to spend more time with are the ones in my unit. Sharing one large living area with twenty-four other men is quite difficult at first. But after a while, I've adjusted to it just fine. That is, if this selection of ward mates remains the same.

There are a few who speak very little, even some that never speak. For those who choose to share conversations and small talk, I have chosen to accept them as respectful individuals. My life experiences, such as college and working in the business world, maybe some musical talent and performance opportunities, make me stick out from everyone else. Even my attire, when I wear my own clothing from home, displays their perception that I have family support, and money.

I'll sometimes have conversations with others about these assets of mine, only because they inquire about it. A few might ask me, "Why are you here? You look like you don't belong here." And they're right, I don't. I've even had guards ask me the same thing, with the same opinion.

To the inmates I have befriended, it is fun hanging out with them. I don't have a choice quite honestly. As a congenial person, I myself choose to spend time with them. Sharing meals, watching TV, playing cards, telling jokes. I have spent more time with them here for the past two weeks than I spent with my best friends from home for the past two years. It's sad to even think about that comparison.

I have come to realize that most of my friendships over the years have been lost. My depression has in some way scared them away, making them uncomfortable with the fact that having a mental illness in the first place is not usually common among others. Perhaps the bonds have been broken because they didn't know how to handle the situation.

Sometimes, I miss them. Other times, I start to forget their names and faces. I guess that's what happens when you forge so many friendships. I consider myself most of the time to be *too* nice and generous, if there is such a thing, but it has brought me positive results.

There are times when I ask myself, "How far will I go to maintain a friendship, not knowing how close and reliable the other individual is?" The answer is truthfully…I don't know. I have been somewhat "screwed over" by past friendships where I felt used. And in some instances, I *was* used. To go out of your way to support your friends, and then be rejected when you need help, doesn't feel good at all.

This happened numerous times, and I was used. I was duped into thinking I might have received *some* support. But a friend should be there for you no matter what, even if they can't help. The recognition of knowing that someone you care about is struggling with something is important, and you can do only what you can to help.

My reaching out to friends, even if it's a cry for help…which is not useful, is usually not the right method of seeking help for any serious matter. I'm not looking for all the answers from them, because they don't have all the answers. But there should some form of understanding, support, and most of all compassion for a friendship to exist. It's another way of saying, "I'm here for you. I'll hold your hand. You'll get through this, and I'll still be here when you overcome what you're struggling with."

When it comes to major depression, and at times suicidal ideations, many are scared. My past friends were scared. As a friend, you can still be helpless. But why abandon a friendship permanently when the problem has nothing to do with you, and you're not expected to fix it?

Things will eventually be resolved, and the distance between these friendships will slowly diminish over time. But I shouldn't throw a meaningful friendship away just because one side of the relationship is temporarily collapsing. If two friends were to hold each end of a rope, it shouldn't be used as a tug-of-war. Instead, it should be used as a jump rope. Let the problems circulate in the middle, jumping up and down, and not be dragged towards one side of a friendship.

Why was I judged by my friends over something that they had nothing to do with? My friends felt uncomfortable knowing that they were friends with someone who was depressed, reaching out using desperate cries for help along with suicidal ideations. It seems that the topic of suicide and depression makes others in general uncomfortable, leading to a point of panic and abandonment. But do you think the person suffering from these depressed feelings deserves the abandonment? No, they don't. As for me, I felt that I didn't deserve to lose the ones I cared about so much.

I am still searching for that spark to reconnect with them. It's ironic to think that these relationships have always been there for me, no matter what I am going through. And yet, I seem to have difficulty reaching out to them. I am afraid of their reaction for my long absence, for the depression ruining my life in the past, and the continuation of our relationship.

What is there to be afraid of, when I know that they're not going anywhere? The day will come when I am reunited with these relationships again, and then they can hear my story, and share it. They wouldn't necessarily share it with others at first. But more importantly, they will share it with me.

I feel like I have abandoned my friends. Friends who I have known for almost my entire life. The more my mind and mental illness persuades me to isolate, the more I miss my friends. I do not intend to continue the friendships I made here when I get released to go home. The friends that have always been there for me are the ones I need to stay with.

I had the chance through other inmates to discover the reason why everyone is here. I was told what crimes they committed, and what mental illness they were suffering from. The crimes were what I was more interested in. When I heard some of the things they mentioned, I was surprised and, in some way, heartbroken. There are some with assault charges, robbery, and even murder.

I get scared when I mention these types of crimes that were committed, knowing that I'm around these dangerous criminals. I don't see that right away when I look at them. They seem so calm, relaxed, and satisfied. But I can tell deep inside they are disappointed and angry.

Some of the inmates imprisoned have been here for years, even decades. I don't know how they do it. How do they adapt to the given living conditions and environment? How do they accept the fact that they're stuck in a dump? Maybe they have nowhere else to live. Their time here is probably better than living out on the streets. I think about their situations, and it makes me more grateful for what I have back at home.

Whatever the situations are for these other inmates, they're still human beings. I spend a lot of time here observing others. The way they talk, speaking with an unethical attitude and tone. When they eat during meals, how the slob inside of them comes out to feast at such a rapid pace on poor quality food. At times, or I should say all the time, trading of side dishes and drinks, desserts and "real" snacks purchased at the convenience store.

Some of them act like they haven't eaten in years. And from some of the stories I've been told about their lives outside of prison, they practically were begging for food. I can tell just by watching them run up to grab their meal trays, as if someone was giving away money. As for the drug addicts here, they would probably take that money and spend it on hard street drugs, like heroin and crack. To them, drugs are the nutritious supplements to nourish their bodies.

The reality of what is available for them outside of prison, is unfortunately the truth. Most of them have nothing, no family, money, friends, a place to live, work, education. Absolutely nothing. Prison for them is a haven. Otherwise, this state and its urban crime cities and streets are all they know. They were raised on the streets, and then arrested on the streets. Vacations and traveling, seeing the world and its wonders, may never be an opportunity for them to experience.

They are stuck here, among the crime and drug infested neighborhoods. A change of environment would do them some good. Unfortunately, they may never have the funds and access to take such a trip. The "streets" is their escape, their paradise. The crimes committed, and the drugs absorbed, are the only available activities.

The more I observe them, and the more I listen to them, my heart gets filled with sadness. My heart grows bigger and bigger, as if the sadness is inflating it like a balloon full of air. And when it pops, my heart sinks deeper into my emotions, and the tears from my eyes begin to fall. It makes me so sad when I combine all the facts about these inmates and their realities. I never experienced what they have gone through and continue to go through.

I see these criminal and mental health patients wasting away in a locked cell. It makes me more upset when I realize that some of them are unaware about themselves, and what they are going through. They look helpless, and content to a point where their movement and facial expressions are that of a zombie.

I don't know what goes on inside their head, and I don't want to know. But it has made me come to realize that these strange people *do* exist. Hearing voices, hallucinating, beliefs in radical ideations, having special powers, have led to one statement, or diagnosis if you're a doctor; they have completely lost their minds.

There's so much hatred here in this facility. Tension between the inmates lurks among the hallways and classrooms. In the units, or living quarters, it depends on the people inside them. The better the unit, in terms of amenities and freedom, the better the inmates.

The hospital will label the units with numbers based on how terrible the living conditions and prisoners are, more so how dangerous they are to themselves and others. The lower numbered wards are the worst, and the rest become tolerable as the numbers increase. The unit I live on, Unit 6, is considered the best unit in the entire facility.

I spent my first three days here in Unit 2 before being transferred to Unit 6. It was unbearable. Everything about it. I was trapped in my cell most of the time, except for meals and showering. And for the time I was out of my room, the other patients were downright disgusting.

They took the meaning of "crazy" to a whole new level. A level that was worse, as if these specific individuals invented it. Screaming and shouting, banging on the door with their firsts and sometimes with their heads, throwing objects such as clothing and food. It was purely a zoo for human beings.

Their hygiene was worse than a dirty dog. Teeth as brown as dirt, with some patients missing a lot of them, dirty long nails, greasy hair and beards, and more acne than a young teenager's face. Some had bruises on their face and head, indicating they were injured during a fight, or the painful marks were self-inflicted. And the tattoos, tattoos seemed like a requirement here, as almost every patient possessed one or more on their body. They were located on arms and hands, necks and faces, torsos and legs.

As I pass by these patients through the hallways, I feel as if I am walking through an art gallery exhibiting criminals. A few of them had gang tattoos, for there are quite a few gangs represented. It's also the reason for why certain colors are not to be worn; red, blue, white, black, yellow. A whole streak of colors unwanted here, like a rainbow of violence. Gray is pretty much the popular and neutral color of choice worn by many, matching their neutral personalities and dull lives.

Fights and arguments occur every hour during the day. Arguing that is started by unnecessary comments and gestures, eventually turning into a quarrel of shoving, pushing, and punching. It can happen to any individual, depending on which type of prisoners you're surrounded by. Even one look, a stare of disgust towards the other, can instigate that person to suddenly attack without reason.

But I have nothing to worry about. I am a nonviolent citizen of society, one who believes that violence does not solve anything. The best tactics I can perform are to keep my head down, focus on my reading and writing, and worry about getting better, rather than unwanted distractions getting in the way.

<u>And Then There Was Joe</u>

""We don't meet people by accident. They are meant to cross our path for a reason." – Unknown

After my very first day here, bunked up in Unit 2 with the craziest of all the looneys imprisoned, I met a fellow inmate who I seemed to get along with. I got along with him very well, because he was just like me...normal.

His name was Joseph, or Joe as he preferred. He was a white male, 37 years old, and served in numerous prisons for nearly half of his life, mostly for aggravated assault charges, some of them occurring in prisons against other inmates and guards.

He also has armed robbery charges pending on his resume for his career in criminal activity. But as I got to know him here, studying his behavior and congeniality, I never saw any of his past anger. Maybe he understood that violence has not helped him but has only caused him more trouble and prison time.

Joe had a good knowledge of how the prison system worked. He knew the ins and outs of what was expected, and how to survive in the more dangerous prisons. Smuggling items from other inmates, even guards, seemed like his specialty. Cigarettes, caffeinated coffee, drugs, pain killers, electronics, and alone time with a female inmate if you're that desperate and willing to take a risk, are just some examples.

Women in prison are not what I am into. Not my preference at all. They looked disgusting, with or without makeup, and their faces looked as if someone smashed them with a baseball bat. I would never touch any of them, even if I wore rubber gloves. And even if you paid me to do it!

But it seemed that Joe didn't mind at all. For a guy that doesn't have great looks, he has the skill to talk with many women in this type of environment, creating relationships for himself. I'm sure a big share of the women he has interacted with during his life were inside prisons.

As I got to know Joe and learn more about his personal life, my thoughts and opinions about him began to change. He told me he had a son, 17 years old, who happened to be the star football player at his high school. Joe's girlfriend, or if she is considered that to Joe anymore, takes care of their son.

He mentions them both sometimes when we talk, but only shares the bare minimum of details. It probably upsets him, knowing that he'd been in prison during his son's entire life so far, barely having any interaction and support for him.

From the way Joe mentions his girlfriend, just by giving her that title in their relationship, I could tell they were never married and do not speak to each other anymore. At times, I wanted to ask Joe if he would take care of his son when finally released from prison. I never had the courage to ask him, but I knew the answer would be "no". He stressed the fact many times that he is disappointed with his life, and that he doesn't want to take care of himself anymore.

His appearance was easy to notice and pick out among dozens of inmates throughout the prison. He was tall, about six feet even, and his body build consisted of a large gut that stuck out, looking like a kickball. His arms were chubby, and his legs built like tree trunks. A lot of his weight, weighing in a total of about 250 pounds, from what he told me, was primarily from his torso and rear end. He walked slow, waddling like a penguin from side to side in slow motion with his arms swaying back and forth.

Joe's hair was shoulder length long, the bottom half in curls glistening with grease. I could never tell when he took a shower, because his hair always looked wet. He had a chubby face covered with facial hair, which was a short beard with several patches of skin and acne. Both his hair and facial hair had spots of gray, and frayed out, as if he was never introduced to a brush or comb.

He had tattoos mostly located on both arms, all in dark blue and black ink. There were no images or designs, only letters. His right forearm had the word "Loyalty" across it. The left arm had scattered letters, possibly initials that have some meaning or representation. His knuckles and top of both hands had initials as well.

The tattoo most noticeable on him was a diamond-shaped teardrop located below his left eye. It was the size of a pebble and could be seen from a distance. As an angry and short-tempered individual, with a history to prove it, I can't imagine him crying with watery tears pouring from his eyes. Even his thick eyebrows, almost connected to form a unibrow, gave a first impression to others that he was grouchy.

But it was his right arm that worried me. From wrist to elbow, on the inside of his arm, were scars. Short and long, faded red lines in all directions. There were about twenty, maybe thirty scars, some thicker than others.

One scar that was the widest and longest was located down the center of his arm. He mentioned to me as he showed it for the first time, that it required 87 stitches. It must have been horrible to go through such an injury, with excruciating pain and large quantity of blood loss, and then being sewn up back together like a rag doll. He remembers this one scar the most, because it almost ended his life.

All the marks down his arm were self-inflicted, with the intention of death. Every scar representing an attempt of suicide, and all with the same failed result. Joe's father committed suicide many years ago, and Joe expressed his obligation to follow his father's footsteps because it ran in his family.

Maybe the help he has received changed his mind, thinking positive about the future and released from prison. Since the day we both moved to Unit 6, our friendship grew stronger, and the trust was solidified with mutual respect. I never expected to have a best friend in prison, but I did.

The Good Things in Prison Life

"One of the many lessons that one learns in prison is, that things are what they are and will be what they will be." – Oscar Wilde

Every late afternoon, while I'm locked away in my cell, I look out my window to watch the sunset. The window is tall in length, but its width is very small, providing me with a limited view. As I look outside, all I see is a small patch of grass, a brown brick building, a large flat top of pavement surrounded by a tall wire fence topped with razor wire, and half of a parking lot full of vehicles, crowded behind the fence in the distance. Overall, not much of a pretty sight to enjoy.

I'm lucky though that I'm able to see the outside world, no matter what the view contains. Looking past the dirty, foggy window, gives me the infrequent calmness that I will soon return to the other side I stare at. The thick, white cement wall covered with pen graffiti, is what divides these two dimensions; the corrupted evil world I am trapped in, and the real world full of freedom, peace and harmony. It would take such a force to bring down this wall I'm stuck behind. This force, in my case, would be utilized as my strength towards recovery, strong enough to break through the thick concrete.

The sunsets make me feel more at ease while I'm locked in my cell. Although my room is located at the end of the hall, tucked away in the corner, I have a perfect view of the sun settling down behind a low tree line. Behind the ugly brick building and congested parking lot, it still looks serene and peaceful.

On a good day, with the right arrangement of clouds, large or small, thick or thin, dark or light, the sunset looks spectacular. A painting perfected with warm colors, derived from a magic palette. Yellow, orange, pink, red, purple. Colors that are dazzling and layered onto each other differently as the sunlight diminishes from the sky. I see different mixtures of these vibrant colors as I gaze out my window every day.

The days where the sunset doesn't appear at all, most likely due to a clouded forecast, I still imagine what it looks like above the ugliness of thick clouds that blanket the sky. At night, before I turn in, I never see the moon or stars. The only lights I see are the bright, fluorescent building and parking lot lamps that highly illuminate the entire compound.

After only one month of living here, I have adjusted to the lifestyle of the ward. I wouldn't call it a "home", but for the time being I'll have to accept it. As each day passes, it becomes more comfortable. In addition, I start to forget the feeling of living in my house, in my room, and in my bed. I spend very little time here in my cell, or room, as opposed to my bedroom at home where I isolate myself all day occupied with TV, video games, and my laptop.

It's different here. This current "house" I'm stuck in contains twenty-four other roommates, some of which I call my friends. If I live here for a long time, then they will become my new family. The security officers will act as our parents, telling us what we can and cannot do. As for the doctors and mental health treatment coordinators, they are the relatives who rarely visit us.

When it comes to creating new relationships, it has certainly been challenging for me. I do realize I am shy at first, but it can be difficult to continue socializing under such pressure and anxiety. The pressure of acceptance is what really bothers me. In a dangerous place like this one, acceptance is what I need to survive here.

First impressions are a vital factor when creating new relationships. It is the ultimate test of whether the other individual will accept and trust you. Trust can be risky to some people if it is broken. When it is broken, it is much harder to regain it from someone who has shattered such a strong bond.

Creating new relationships, and maintaining the existing ones, is off balance when compared on a scale. For me, I have focused too much on creating new ones, not paying attention to my existing ones that I should be cherishing more. And as time goes on without the communication with existing relationships, they start to diminish, and fade away.

Isolation has been my best friend for many years. It has acted as my companion in times of need. It was not the wisest decision and partner to take. I pushed myself away from others, even family, to comfort myself alone and without any interruptions. Over time, it felt normal for me. The irony is that I also feel alone enough to express desperation for others to be by my side.

But isolation in a psychiatric prison is like asking for more trouble. I need to be surrounded by others, feeling safe among those who I have come to trust during my time here. Without interaction, I think I might go insane like the rest of the prisoners here. My time here needs to pass quickly, and communication with the criminally insane is my only way of making it happen.

I have trouble meeting others when out in public. Finding a topic of discussion to strike up the conversation has been my challenge. What do I say, and how do I carry on the conversation? I do the same thing when I talk to those I already know. No matter who the other person is that I'm attempting to speak with, my conversation skills need a lot of work. If I didn't isolate so much, my practice could progress much more quickly.

I proved myself wrong during my time here so far. Successful with making temporary friendships to make my stay here more comfortable, I got more than what I asked for. My ward mates have been like brothers to me. They always watch my back and prevent other inmates from giving me a hard time. That's what brothers are for, right? Protection?

They give me a tremendous amount of respect, return it back to them in kind. Most of them are aware of my intelligence and education, and perhaps that is the reason for them to look up to me. For some, I am a role model, a teacher to educate them with the knowledge and skills they have never learned before.

From what I've observed, it's difficult for them to learn the material I am teaching.

The lessons I instruct seem to confuse them more than they already are. They are eager to learn, thinking how I'm the nicest teacher they've ever had, and for some of them, the only teacher they've ever had. I can tell just from the look in their eyes, they're struggling and more disappointed with themselves.

When it comes to meals here, everyone acts in a panic. A good panic, that is. As the cell doors unlock, the instant when they slowly creak open with just inches of space, everyone hurries out of their room in a frenzy. Doors slam open, and they sprint towards the entrance of the ward, as if there was a fire spreading throughout the building. Bumping into each other and cutting the line, the hectic crowd of hungry men leap and grasp for their food trays like it was their last meal of their lives. I was in no rush. I would usually wait to be the last one handed their meal.

Food preparation and quality, in terms of taste and presentation, was horrific. At every meal, as I lift my tray cover and discover what slop was given, I always state to others, "I've had better. Much better." And trust me, I have. But what could I do? I couldn't starve myself half of the time, while feeding on candy bars and cookies once a day. I tolerated the food, and my digestive system kept complaining.

Visiting hours are considered a rare, family luxury for many patients. I say that because most of them barely have any form of contact with their own family members, and mostly parents. For some patients, they have no idea where their parents are, if they're still alive. And for those reasons, having a visitor never occurs during their time spent here.

My parents were the only ones who come to visit me. There are window visits, where I am face to face with thick glass dividing myself from my visitors. Communication is transferred through a phone, with poor sound quality, and other patients surrounding me with booming loud voices. I tried this method the first time I had visitors, and it was not pleasant. Not even worth a visit, as it is already a hassle for my parents to drive almost 2 hours for a 30-minute visiting session.

My other option was contact visits, where I can hug my parents and sit with them at a table, like normal people would have a conversation. Each time I hugged them, it made me feel like I was home again. My arms wrap around them tight, giving me the sense that everything was going to be fine. In addition to these visits, my parents could bring me food. And I mean "real" food.

Although the "real" food I received was fast food and snacks, it was more real than the disgusting food I ate here. I would be upset for a moment after they left. This feeling passed instantly, as I knew the following nights I would talk to them on the phone. Constant communication from my parents made my time here much easier, and I was extremely grateful to be so lucky.

Time for School

"Learning never exhausts the mind." – Leonardo da Vinci

Every week, Monday through Friday, all patients are required to participate in what is called Rehab Classes. Four periods, each an hour long, with two in the morning and two in the afternoon. The first half of the day is treated like high school. Commuting from class to class as patients, or students in this case, roaming the hallways talking to each other and hanging out as much as they can before the next class begins.

Attendance is taken by the teachers. Those who are not present in their assigned class are hunted down by guards throughout the entire facility. That's right…the entire hospital, as if there was an attempted escape. Other patients linger in the hallways attempting to get inside classrooms they are not assigned to.

Overall, it's pretty much an unorganized imitation of a school. Most of the classrooms make it look like an elementary school, with motivational posters and children's drawings plastered on the walls. As for the patients, or students, they really do have the education and though process of a small, innocent child.

My schedule of classes was very helpful, making me more productive. I first had Library, where you are basically stuck and crammed in a small, crowded room surrounded by book shelves. There were several activities to do; read from a selection of newspapers from the local and Tri-State area, read a book, listen to music, or watch TV. I always spent the period writing in my notebook while listening to music.

Small radios with headphones, almost as old as I am, were available to sign out and use. Not only were they old, but they had poor reception when trying to find a radio station from the limited selection of channels available. There was a classical music station I listened to, relaxing me while I ponder through my thoughts and tune out the unnecessary noise around me. It was really the only opportunity I had to listen to this genre of music I enjoy very much, also making me miss it more to play with a symphony.

The great thing the library had to offer was checking out books, a very rare convenience for many patients. Most of the books are too advanced for patients, based on their low reading level and lack of education. I could check out one book at a time, I would finish reading it within three or four days. It was like my own personal library to use, because I was the only one using it.

The books were categorized; fiction, non-fiction, business, religion, spirituality, and autobiographies. I stuck with fiction novels, to entertain myself through some form of media, and business books to expand my business knowledge and education from college. Their selection of business was very small. More like two or three books total. So, I did what many did not have access or funds for; order a dozen books from Amazon.

They were all business books, with the help of my mother selecting and shipping them out to me. I read through them all within a few weeks, as it consumed almost all my spare time here. And it helped a lot. Not only with passing the time here but making me more eager to get back to my business career in Marketing.

The same activity and time spent for other patients was something perfect for the library…sleeping. While others watched the booming loud television, showing a horrible action or Kung-Fu movie that was poorly downloaded and burned onto a DVD, everyone else was sleeping as if they hadn't slept in days.

The sounds of snoring, light and heavy, would battle with the TV volume and shake the tables. A few would have their heads down on the table, some slumped back in their chairs, and some would sit in the corner and cocoon themselves under their jackets. It wasn't a library. It was a nursery for grown men. The librarian never once shushed anyone.

My second period class was Gym, and the class name basically explains what it was. A big gymnasium, a blue full-court basketball floor with several rows of stadium-style seats on one side, and a small stage with tables and chairs on the other. There was also a weight room at the end with exercise bikes and weight machines, which was hardly used. Several patients would shoot the basketball around, maybe a few would play a game on one side of the court.

The small stage was designated for guards to lounge and play cards, and in the rows of seats, a combination of patients sitting and dozing off. Sleeping seemed to be the common activity shared around here, as some would even sleep on the sides of the gym floor, occasionally struck by bouncing basketballs. Exercise was highly encouraged to patients, and some would spend the period by walking around the gym. Otherwise, just another snooze-fest opportunity for everyone.

The afternoon classes were more productive and in small classrooms. Third period for me was Art Therapy, an activity I enjoyed that very much made me relax. Unfortunately, there were still distractions. It was in a large activity room, shared with another class. Art Therapy had drawings and pictures available to color in during the period. Believe it or not, it was a class in which everyone participated. Not only was the activity relaxing to all, but it was an opportunity for patients to create something artistic and keep it as memorabilia to remember their time here.

The class had a teacher, who was very helpful and supportive. Her name was Allison, a young woman in her thirties. She had long blonde hair, thick black glasses, and a smile that would flash towards patients, letting them know that everything is calm and peaceful. Even the shoes she always wore were artsy, a collaboration of splattered bright colors resembling a tie-dyed shirt. For most of the class time, she would sit in the corner taking notes, and at times sharpen colored pencils for those who requested it.

I enjoyed coloring mandalas, which are very detailed symmetrical designs intended to create a calm, stress-free environment during the coloring process. They are very common among adults, as there are hundreds of different adult coloring books located in bookstores to help alleviate stress. Coloring in this class was not only to rid me of my own stress, but to get me out of this hellhole quicker. It was one of the many ongoing activities during my daily routine here that made the time go quicker.

My last class was Life-Learning Management. The name of the class was obvious as to what we learned. Cooking, playing games, a little history, and teamwork were just some of the topics we addressed. I purposely took this class for the other half of what we focused on learning; personal coping skills and how to manage our problems outside of prison life. It was something I needed to participate and be educated on, no matter how advanced the class was, which it wasn't.

For myself, I learned topics that I already acquired from various inpatient and outpatient programs in the past. But this time around it seemed different. It was a class full of convicts and violent men who have not been accustomed to this type of self-help education. No matter what the settings were for this group, I had to take it seriously for my own sake.

The teacher, Stephanie, oversaw running the group. She was more of an occupational therapist, and so were the other teachers in the facility. She did an exemplary job, above and beyond in order to help everyone on an individual basis.

She had tan skin, most likely from her Middle-Eastern descent, long golden-brown curly hair, and a bright smile you could see from a far distance. Her attitude and tone were very friendly with the patients, as if she was more like a friend rather than a teacher. It was unexpected coming from someone who was very attractive and high maintenance, surrounded by dangerous criminals.

Sandy had a lot of good things to say and gave a high level of respect to everyone. This was the one class that felt like a class; quiet, productive, and full of attention from the students. A classroom etiquette particularly like this one is something you rarely see from all the rehab classes here throughout each day.

I never enjoyed my morning classes of Library and Gym. I felt I was not in an environment where I could be more productive. The library was more of a recreational room, which the Rehabilitation Center already had, with a choice of two activities: sleeping or watching a movie. The only benefit of the library was to check out books. But after several weeks with twenty books read, the selection to me was boring.

I decided to order books from Amazon, so I could read more on what I studied in business school; marketing, advertising, consumer behavior, and economics. In addition, I ordered books to help me with my decision-making skills and coping with depression. My room, a room with my desk, sink, toilet, and bed, was now my library.

Gym class offered very little to be productive. Sleeping and playing cards were my only options, and I chose not to participate in either one. It was time to make some adjustments.

The process of switching classes was doable, but not so much reliable. It was rather easy, for all you had to do was ask for a small pink form, or as they call it "the pink slip", fill it out and return it to any teacher or rehab coordinator. Sounds easy, doesn't it? In fact, I found it more annoying, depending on who you gave it to, determined how long the form took to arrive in the right hands to approve it.

I tried numerous times, sometimes finding out weeks later that the form was never handed in. I was aware of the rules and regulations involved to have it approved, but my patience was growing thin. My persistence finally worked, and my morning classes were changed to my liking.

Library during first period was changed to Current Events. It was a small class setting and was ironically much quieter than the library. Plus, I enjoyed talking about what's going on in the world during the present, rather than reading books about the world from the past. Although I watched the news on TV throughout the day and read the newspapers daily, discussing it with the group and listening to others' opinions was more intriguing.

There were rarely discussions, because no one spoke. Maybe it was because they didn't understand what was going on around the world, outside of prison life. Perhaps they chose not to participate because they didn't want to be part of the outside world, among society as just another civilian living a normal life. Their world had been prison, and the news they discussed was about other prisoners.

My teacher for the class was named Randy, the same individual who helped me create my rehab class schedule when I first arrived here. He gave me some basic skills and reading comprehension tests to evaluate my knowledge and offer a selection appropriate classes to choose from.

With my high level of education, compared to just about every single prisoner in this facility, I completed all the tests with nothing but perfect scores. I probably even set a Guinness World Record for the fastest time to finish these tests specifically for this rehabilitation center I call a joke.

Randy was a Caucasian male, most likely in his late 40s, whose body figure was so skinny I thought he was a cancer survivor. He had a lot of energy, and was always upbeat, pacing quickly around the classroom as if he had twenty Red Bulls.

His humor was his main tool for communicating to the class, which was terrible and extremely corny. If only I could speak in the language of "terrible jokes", I would respond back and have a conversation with him.

As he tried constantly to make me laugh, I tried even harder to make myself laugh at all. The only time I really laughed was when he made jokes about President Donald Trump. Laughing about President Trump? I mean, who hasn't? Nonetheless, Randy was a nice individual who always tried his best to make everyone participate and enjoy the class.

Second period, which used to be Gym, was changed to Horticulture. I have hardly had any experience attempting to be a botanist in my life, but the description of this class sounded better than sleeping on a cold basketball court. The class was held in the same classroom as Current Events and Life-Learning Management.

Randy was my teacher as well this period, and I was certain he was not an actual botanist during his life. But from what I learned, his knowledge on plants and gardening was adequate for a group of prisoners who are not allowed to go outside.

One side of the classroom consisted of about two dozen plants, different shapes and sizes with names I've never even heard of. It was not quite the "Garden of Eden", but more so like the "Garden of Prison". There was even a large greenhouse outside the classroom used during the warmer seasons to grow fruits and vegetables. Occasionally, the food grown in the greenhouse would be used to cook a meal or snack during class. It was the month of January, and the greenhouse looked abandoned and rundown, surrounded by a barbwire fence.

Inside the classroom, there was a large fish tank next to the potted plants. It was very well-decorated, with beautiful plants and fake coral reef, along with a few tiny underwater structures and houses. The tank had two small fish, both the size of a penny. It was always hard to look for them through the glass, for the tank was big enough to hold at least fifty fish.

Randy would always start both classes with a "How are you feeling today?" scale, ranging from one to five. Each prisoner would come up to the front of the class and write their initials with their number next to it on a large whiteboard. After everyone had gone, including Randy himself, the class would together add up all the numbers listed on the board. When the total was calculated, it would then be divided by the number of participants to find the class average for the day.

It was quite pathetic to see everyone have difficulty with such simple math they learned back in elementary school, if they even learned it at all. By the time they started to add up all the numbers, I had already had the class average calculated in my head in just a matter of seconds. As I would shout out the correct average every time we begin to calculate it, heads immediately turned to me as if I was just blurting out random numbers.

At the end, when we finally found out the correct answer, which happened to be my accurate answer earlier, heads turned toward me in shock, and they thought I was a genius. Seeing everyone else struggle with this daily routine, I would not trust any of them to work behind a cash register.

<u>There's No Crying in Prison</u>

"It opens the lungs, washes the countenance, exercises the eyes, and softens down the temper; so cry away." – Charles Dickens

Lately, during the past few months, I've noticed that I cry more often than I have for the past few years. I can tell that the depression is getting heavier, deep inside of me. It covers me like a warm blanket, comforting me. As it continues to swallow me whole, it swarms throughout my body with feelings of numbness and discomfort.

There are moments when I can feel my thoughts suddenly shift moods in an instant without my control. As if a lightning bolt struck my head, clouding my mind with darkness. My judgement is taken over by such a devastating force, while my emotions are frozen in a state of negativity.

What overbears me, is the sensational feeling whenever I cry. I say "sensational", because it transforms me into a completely different person where it feels better having such release.

Depending on the mood, on the thoughts, the teardrops run down my cheeks at a different pace. My eyes begin to water. The sacks of water behind my eyelids fill up quickly, making my eyes red and heavy. And when that moment comes, that climactic second when everything you feel has fallen apart, a single waterfall drops down as thin as string. Every thought that saddens me creates a new drop to fall. One after another, they continue to drop on command.

It's hard to tell when it stops, or what makes it stop. I don't think there's a magic word or phrase that stops it. It all depends on the right moment, when you feel these emotions have disappeared. I feel much better after this brief session of depression has passed. But it's only temporary. I anticipate that the following day it will happen once again, even without any warning letting me know it's about to begin.

At this point, I would consider it as a daily ritual, a habit or a ritual.

Whenever I cry, it is usually over the same topics in my life. The thoughts are about the people I have lost or been distant from for quite some time. I get more upset when I think about my family, the way I let them down with my actions and mistakes, and how I deal with my mental illness.

These past few months, I haven't dealt with it correctly. This has made my family more stressed. Each time I have an episode, they feel helpless. The more it occurs, the less my family interacts with me.

In prison, crying is not an option when amongst others. I never saw anyone else besides myself cry. These were real men. Men who chose not to cry to show off their intimidation and dangerous character traits about themselves. Crying is for wimps, they thought. But do real men cry? Yes, they do.

I saw myself as a man, but one who gets in touch with their feelings and is not afraid to display their emotions. In some ways, crying is healthy to those who have been struggling with depression, bottling in their thoughts and feelings. People wonder why it feels good after you cry. It's because you've let everything out of your system, expressing yourself and knowing that you have accomplished this necessary task.

It can't go on forever, but the temporary state for whatever we need to cry about helps us through that moment. Why fake it, when we can make it? There is no shame in making it happen when it comes to crying. The shame is on others who judge you for expressing yourself.

Each teardrop represents a thought that is poured out from your mind. There sometimes may be just that one single teardrop that falls down our face. One teardrop is all it may take, for that teardrop could be such a big thought troubling your mind. And if multiple teardrops appear? Then it may be proof that many thoughts were troubling us.

Sometimes, my tears gather up in my eyelids like buckets of water. I then make the decision on whether to let these troubling thoughts go and let them run down my cheeks. There have been times here in this psychiatric prison, where crying is unheard of, where I chose to let my tears go. But most of the time, only because it was too hard to cry in this environment, the sacks of water would dry up or fall back behind my eyes.

There were moments when I cried in front of other inmates. They were shocked, surprised at the fact that men could cry. Yes, of course they can. And as for me, I wasn't ashamed of it. It let others at the prison know, even the guards, that I was having sad and depressing feelings. That I was battling something deep inside of myself, and I was sent to this psychiatric prison for a reason.

They knew I wasn't crazy, but they knew depression got the worse of me. My actions of getting myself in trouble and sent here were due to my impulsivity and poor choices. Because of one impulsive, poor choice that I made during an emotional episode, I was committed to a psychiatric prison as a result of my crimes.

I was sent here to receive treatment, and I took advantage of that. My crying was accepted here by my fellow inmates, because they knew how strong of an individual I was wanting to get better and move on with my life. And so, I continued throughout my time in this facility to cry it out, making it rain down my face.

<u>Part II</u>

Journal from the Depths of Darkness

The following date entries are based on true events. These events occur chronologically, from beginning to end of my journey.

Some material may be inappropriate to read, so please skip ahead if you are uncomfortable.

For the privacy of those in this next section, their names have been altered.

An Unexpected Start

November 30, 2017:

"Be willing to have it so. Acceptance of what has happened is the first step to overcoming the consequences of any misfortune." – William James

It all began with a knock.

From the sound of it, it was more like banging on the door. Continuous banging, as each bang became louder. I was startled by this as it woke me up. I turned over in my bed to check the time. Six-thirty in the morning. I was confused. Who would come so early to disturb my family and me?

There was a feeling in my stomach that didn't agree with me. A nervous feeling, making me anxious and filling me with fear. Something was not right, and I could immediately tell just by the constant banging on the door. I rolled out of bed and hurried to my window. My mouth and eyes widened as I looked outside.

Ten cop vehicles, at least. I didn't have time to count how many there were parked sporadically in front of my house. Panic filled my body as my eyes gazed at the horror outside. Dozens of police officers gathered as a mob on my driveway, standing around, waiting for what was about to happen next.

I heard my mother answer the front door. I tried to hear the conversation, but all I heard was my mother calmly letting the people at the door inside. I ran back to my room, and quickly put on the nearest clothes in sight. I closed my door and sat on my bed waiting. My body was trembling. I was shaking so hard I thought I was going to pass out and fall to the ground. My heart felt like it was ready to pop at any moment. I expected a loud knock on my door, but there was nothing yet.

I slowly approached my door and opened it. After I took several steps outside of my room, two officers grab me and threw me to the ground inside of my room. "On the ground, on the ground! Don't move!", they said repeatedly. They kept repeatedly yelling it so many times, as if they thought I had a hearing problem or didn't understand English. How could I move, or get myself to the ground? These two officers had done the job already for me by throwing me on the ground, handcuffing my hands behind my back. I couldn't move, and I could barely breathe.

For some strange reason, I wasn't having a panic attack as would be expected in a situation like this one. Instead, I expected for this day to eventually come, already aware that I had done something wrong in the recent past. And now it's finally here. It had been two months since the crime was committed, and at this precise moment I wish it was longer.

As I was pulled up from the ground and placed sitting on my bed, more police officers entered my bedroom. A detective I had been interrogated by before, about a month ago, came into my room, and sat on my desk chair in front of me. "I told you this day would come.", he said. I leaned forward, with a serious look, and said to him, "I told you I shouldn't even be alive right now." Although this criminal act was originally planned as a suicide, the attempt failed and led to my being in trouble instead.

For the next few minutes, I was explained the situation and what would happen next. It was followed by my Miranda Rights being read to me, along with signing some documents. As this was going on, I looked to the right on the ground and saw my dog sitting there silently.

She was barely moving, hence the reason why I didn't even notice her there in the first place. The detective continued to speak to me as I stared at my dog. She was scared, just like me. I could feel her pain and nervousness as she stared back at me. She knew something was wrong.

Whenever something is wrong with me, she can somehow sense it, and will come to my side to comfort me. I couldn't even pat her on the head or put my arm around her due to being handcuffed. And I wanted to so badly. I was scared, wanting some form of support and comfort in this terrifying situation. Even if I could, it wouldn't be enough to fix this dilemma.

After this "meeting" concluded, I was escorted down the stairs and into the office room, as my family called it, located right by the front door. I sat on a couch inside of the room, still handcuffed and scared out of my mind. Two police officers were standing guard in front of me, staring at me. They gently rested one of their hands onto their guns, cautious and alert. Did they really think I was going to do something, like run away? Where would I go? I wouldn't even make it more than five feet out of the room.

In the dining room right outside of the office, my mother sat with the detective at a table, talking about what was going to happen to me next. I sat there waiting, shaking my head in shame and disgust with myself. I should be dead, I thought. This wasn't supposed to happen to me. I should be six feet under, with my family and friends still mourning for me.

The two officers continued to stare at me, probably thinking that I'm now scum and a worthless human being. I stared at them and softly said to them, "Kill me. Just kill me…please." They looked at each other, confused. "I want to die.", I stated as tears rolled down my face. One of the officers finally spoke. "Why?", he responded. "Trust me, you don't want to end your life right now." Obviously, he doesn't know me too well.

"Don't you want me to die?", I asked. No response. I could tell my begging and pleading for my death was annoying them. They probably thought I was doing this for attention. But if they really knew me, or at least some of my history of my depression and suicidal ideations, they would have taken the situation more seriously. I stopped talking after several minutes, and then the time arrived.

The two officers helped me up, and I was taken outside through the front door of the house. I noticed a black, metal police battering ram next to the front door. Would they really go that far just to retrieve me? Apparently so. I walked toward the mob scene set up outside of my house of police vehicles and officers. The officers escorting me placed me in one of the dozens of cop cars surrounding my house.

I looked around my neighborhood to see if anyone was outside watching. No one in sight. It was still very early in the morning, but I knew someone was probably watching. Someone is always watching. And what a show I was giving them. Better than what they've probably seen from cop reality shows on TV. The car started driving away from my house, and I was on my way to the police station.

When I arrived there, I was placed inside of an interrogation room. The detective entered the room, same one who spoke to at my house, and asked me more questions. As I sat there, I slowly attempted to cut my wrists with the tight handcuffs strapped on them. He noticed and ordered for me to stop. And so, I did.

It was my way of telling him that I wanted to die, like the two officers who were guarding me at my house. I needed to show him my urgency for dying. He stopped questioning me and took me out of the room to get fingerprinted and processed.

During these procedures, I continued trying to cut my wrists at various times when I could and repeated saying suicidal statements. No response, and no reaction. I was surprised, thinking that the police would do anything in their power to prevent me from these horrible actions. I had no luck with cutting my wrists with the handcuffs, which instead left a giant red bruise on top of my hands and wrists.

After being at the police station for two hours, I was then taken by ambulance to a nearby hospital. It was decided that because of my suicidal statements and actions displayed towards the police officers, that I be admitted into an emergency room.

Well, it wouldn't be my first time going through this process. This is probably trip number sixteen, or seventeen. I couldn't even keep track anymore because of so many emergency rooms visit I have experienced due to suicidal ideation.

This trip was different though. I was a prisoner, escorted and guarded by police officers, handcuffed to the stretcher. I arrived at the emergency room and was rolled inside to a room. I guess this was the first stop on my journey to wherever I was going to end up. Jail? Prison? A psychiatric hospital? Home?

There were so many questions running through my mind. One after another, piling on top of each other and giving me a headache. But I didn't have the answers to any of these questions. Not one single answer. I was clueless, confused, and most of all…hopeless.

<u>Welcome to Prison</u>

December 4, 2017:

*"America is the land of the second chance -
and when the gates of the prison open, the
path ahead should lead to a better life." –*
George W. Bush

The unbearable time stuck in the same hospital bed, staring at the limited view and madness of the ER, had come to an end. This moment was what I dreaded for the past five days while waiting in the emergency room. I had no idea where I was going next, where they were taking me to be locked up and evaluated by doctors. At least, that's what I was expecting.

There had to be some decency of treating such an individual with a mental illness, even though a crime has been committed. I was hoping for the consequences to not be so severe, and instead to have the time spent reflecting on what I did wrong, and how I could make myself better again.

As the stretcher approached my hospital room, I knew it was time to go and move onto the next phase of this nightmare. I was strapped in with leather straps, my hands and ankles handcuffed to the metal bars on the side. It was cold outside, after all it was nearly winter, and I had two white blankets wrapped around me like a burrito. The blankets hid the straps and handcuffs, concealing my new identity as a prisoner.

I would have been embarrassed to have every set of eyes stare at me as they rolled me down the corridor. But that didn't matter. When you have three police officers and detectives escorting you out of the hospital, it doesn't help hide the shame and embarrassment.

It was night time, and I was being loaded into an ambulance. The bitter cold air was the first time I breathed fresh air in almost a week. The air struck my lungs hard as I briefly breathed it in, adding to the internal pain I was already suffering from during this transition. I was told the ride to where I was going, which I still was not told, was almost a two-hour ride. Great. Stuck in a cold ambulance, tightly strapped to a stretcher.

I could barely move to begin with, and the only part of my body that moved the entire trip were my eyes. They glanced curiously around the ambulance, and up at the roof. And for several moments during this road trip to hell, my eyes went through the motion of watering and pouring out my anticipated sadness.

After two hours of a bumpy ambulance ride, I finally arrived at my destination. From what I could see as I was being unloaded from the ambulance, I saw dark gray brick buildings with bright fluorescent lights shining everywhere, blinding my current whereabouts. I had the sense already that this was a prison.

Where else would they send me? I wasn't expecting any five-star hotel or any luxury in-patient hospital where you were treated with respect. This was pure hell, and I was about to enter its gates.

The officers dropped me off like a package, as they rang the front doorbell and left me at the door without saying anything. I was then taken into a small room where for the next half hour I was evaluated by the facility's medical director. He asked the usual questions to learn about me, my past medical history and such. I could tell by his yawning and unenthusiastic attitude that he didn't want to be here. Besides, it was one o'clock in the morning. Who would want to be doing this at such a late hour?

After the evaluation was complete, I undressed and took a quick-freezing cold shower next to the evaluation room. My clothes were taken, and all I was given as I got out of the shower was a robe as heavy as a rug. I wasn't even given a towel to dry myself off. The robe barely covered my body, and I was then escorted down the hall. The hallways were quiet and dark, if everyone was sleeping. At least, that's what I thought.

As I entered the unit I, I heard screaming and banging from other inmates. I was right...this was hell. My freezing, wet body continued to drip down the hallway, and I arrived at my cell. A rubber mat, with no sheets and pillow, and a steel toilet that looked as if one hundred men just used it recently. I was trapped.

I knew to expect such a living condition that was disgusting and uncomfortable. I had a guard sit in my doorway, for I was on constant watch, in case I were to do something harmful to myself. I couldn't sleep at all, and my thoughts were constantly racing with fear, with no hope in sight. I knew I had really screwed up this time, and now I'm living the reality of what I feared the most…living as a prisoner.

December 7, 2017:

"It is only through labor and painful effort, by grim energy and resolute courage, that we move on to better things." – Theodore Roosevelt

For the past two days, I have been living in the worst unit of the facility, Unit 2. All new inmates, or "patients" according to the doctors here, were placed in this unit upon their arrival. There's only one word I can use to describe this unit: hell. That's right. Hell. It's a little much for a description of an environment, considering no one knows what hell is *really* like. But I can imagine it being like what I'm living with right now.

Most of the other inmates are locked in their cell the entire time. They never come out, unless they're ready to…or even want to. Some of these prisoners are like caged monkeys, throwing food and their own shit around, jumping around making obscene noises and gestures. There was even one prisoner who was always naked, screaming at his locked cell door while banging on his chest. I guess he was the gorilla in this barrel of monkeys mess I was stuck in.

I highly doubted any miracles occurred here, but today I was wrong. A miracle happened to me, as it was announced I'd be moving to the best unit in the entire prison. I still didn't know what that meant, considering this *was* a prison. But when I arrived in my new living quarters, Unit 6, I was relieved. This truly was a miracle!

The unit was practically silent. No one was screaming at the top of their lungs or banging their head against the door. Even the unit was clean, without the stench of body odor and shit, something I dealt with back in Unit 2. It was somewhat civilized here in this unit. This could work for me, and for someone of my caliber, I deserved it. My journey will continue here, and hopefully not for much longer.

I entered my new room, and before they locked me in my cell, I asked for a pen and paper to keep myself busy in the meantime. A guard came back with my request, he shut my door, and it was time for me to get acquainted with my new surroundings.

Now that I was able to do some writing, what do I write about? I had no idea what to write. The only thing I could think about was my future, and how this current situation could ruin it.

I worked so hard to get to where I currently am. My education, work experience, musical talent, and the skills of teaching and learning. It's all put on hold at this current moment. The only question is; how do I get it all back?

I always had intentions of living a good life. One that is decent and satisfactory to my standards. A life that will bring me joy and success. The only life to suffice myself of the good things this world has to offer is at jeopardy.

On the bright side, I still have plenty of life left to live. I just need to think positively about what the future holds for me. Who knows, maybe great achievements are in store for me. What we do in this life, is what makes our outcomes possible to reach any level of certainty. But how do we know if we are doing enough?

Maybe this unfortunate experience will open new opportunities for me in the future, and I can accomplish things I never thought of doing in my life. What if I wrote a book? Writing a book was never in the game plan for my future, but I'm inspired to share my experience through writing. Writing is what's going to get me past this journey. It'll keep me alive.

It's important for me to always keep busy. And I will continue to do so. The assortment of activities I partake in will not matter. What *will* matter, is to pursue this goal of writing and publishing this book so I can keep on living, enjoying what life has to offer. If you're reading this book right now, it means I achieved my goal.

<u>My Start to Recovery</u>

December 11, 2018:

"Our prisons and our jails are now our mental health institutions." – Hillary Clinton

Today I met with my psychologist for the first time. Every inmate in this facility is assigned to a psychologist, and I could tell just from my observations that no one wanted a doctor speaking with them. These one-on-one meetings between doctors, social workers, and inmates would occur in a large meeting room with two officers guarding the door.

There were about ten tables, with small wall dividers bordering each table area. The dividers were meant for privacy reasons, although I always heard loud voices arguing around me in the room from the other inmates. It seemed that this time for inmates to discuss problems with their doctor was instead utilized to scream at them and call them inappropriate names. The way I saw it was that these inmates didn't think they could be helped. So instead, they rejected the help whenever it was available.

As for me, I want to get out of here as soon as possible. For me to do that, cooperation with treatment and working with my doctors here was necessary. And of course, I wanted the help. I didn't want to end up worse than where I am now. When I expressed my eagerness and dedication to my psychologist about getting better, something happened unexpectedly.

My psychologist called over two people from the other side of the room. They came over, sat down, and introduced themselves. Two more psychologists. Now I was getting nervous. Was it something I said?

The three doctors explained to me that they wanted to give me extra treatment during my stay here. I was confused at first, but as they further explained the situation it became clearer. They *really* wanted to help me. It was as if we had some mindful connection, informing us that I didn't belong here. And they knew it. I knew it.

An offer was made at the table. That sounds as if we were doing a business deal here, but this is my life we're talking about here, so it *did* mean business. The three of them would meet with me three times a week for one hour. Wow…sounds intriguing.

So, what was the catch? There was none. It was explained to me that this offer was a rarity here at this facility. The usual routine is meeting with one psychologist, once a week, for only fifteen minutes. I was told that majority of the inmates turn down this opportunity and don't even last more than a minute. They sit down, scream and curse at the doctor, and exit the room still screaming and cursing.

The fact that I was given this offer made me feel special, privileged in a place where privileges are also a rarity. It was because these three doctors I was staring at knew I wanted the help, and that they were willing to put in the extra time to help me. One of the doctors simply said to me, "We see a lot of potential in you. We have confidence that you will receive the treatment you need here with us. You've been talking with the three of us for almost an hour now, and you haven't screamed, cursed at us, and left the session. That tells us something, and it shows who you really are." Nice little speech there, I guess. It basically just meant, "You're a normal, sane individual, and we'd like to help."

I accepted the offer, and for the next several weeks I would be discussing my life with these three psychologists. They would also get more attention from someone in that one hour than they do the entire day they're at the prison. It was a win-win situation.

A lot of people tell me I still have my whole life ahead of me. I agree with them to a certain degree, but it is I who needs to be confident with this statement. With this harsh event in my life, it is time to start re-planning my future.

What will I do with myself? How will I extend my professional career path? What steps do I need to take in rebuilding my social life? There are many areas that need to be updated. The process of getting there is what stands in my way. Everything in life is a process, and the approach towards it will decide the completion of it.

Deep within my heart, I truly do want to feel better. I need to get better. It needs to be my top priority among the other necessities I require. Making myself better is what I consider to be a full-time job. My life needs to have the highest capacity of positive energy and emotion. A complete reversal of my life, from the "downs" to the "ups", needs to occur.

One thing I need to focus on is taking the first step towards recovery. My only question is, where do I begin? Taking the first step can be hard. An approach to taking the first step towards anything really, is difficult. In my case, it's one small step to get to the beginning, and one giant leap to get to the end.

Like I mentioned before, everything is a process. You take it one step at a time, and always keep moving forward. Any trips or sudden falls can alter your walk down the path to victory. If that's the metaphor describing having my life back, then I assume the reward should be in the form of a trophy. Maybe a certificate. But it should not come down to those options. Gaining my life back to the level that satisfies me is the greatest reward, with high quality and true value. It all depends on reaching that vital obstacle.

I question myself a lot as to why dealing with depression, and getting my life back together, is such a long process. At times, I feel impatient when trying to get what needs to get done. And majority of these occurrences relate to my mental health treatment. I wish my problems could be fixed with a snap of my fingers, or by saying a magic word. But it doesn't work like that.

Applying my eagerness in wanting to get better can be difficult because I know it is going to be a lot of hard, time consuming work. So, then the eagerness goes away, making it more difficult to gain it back. The motivation fueled by eagerness diminishes over time, and then I'm stuck back at where I began.

The approach towards treating depression can be a process. Steps need to be taken to have the realization that you *are* indeed going through some tough times. Many choose not to accept or believe it, but perhaps that is the first step to this process: acceptance. Once the acceptance is there, the next step of laying out your options for treatment is implemented. Now, these options can vary depending on the individual. Some more intensive than the others. But it's necessary, and we've already established that with the first step of acceptance.

Brainstorming your options of how to make yourself better is necessary, and I say "brainstorming" because this is a project that needs so much planning ahead. It's all about your life, and how you're going to continue living it out with a positive outlook. This is a project that needs to get done, and the process of taking it step by step is important. The wait is worth it, because you are worth it.

Throughout my journey to recovery, I need to stay strong the entire time. Strength is as strong as its meaning. To sustain this "strength", I must concentrate on the tasks that need to be completed. It is the strength, deep within myself, that will carry me.

The absence of strength will make me weak. My actions will be uncontrollable. During these moments, the consequences will be severe. It is as if this strength symbolizes a shield, surrounding me. This shield of mine cannot be penetrated or broken. And at any moment, when I turn my back on this protection, I will be defenseless...and helpless.

But where does this strength derive from? How do I find it to survive? The characteristics of this strength I continue to search for is measured only by its mentality, not by the physicality viewed from the outside. Strength, applied with mindfulness, will lift my spirits and make me continue living. The repetition to practice mindfulness will work with full effort, and without any periods of ease.

Just like any ordinary gym, one must decide how much weight they can handle when lifting. Sometimes we know what we can handle, because we're used to how our bodies are growing stronger. In this case, strength is not measured by mass, but by how mindful you are to get yourself through whatever obstacle needs to be challenged. And just like most gyms, there is no judgement.

How much weight can our mind handle? What does it take to lift our heads high, and look forward to success? Will it get easier as we walk further down the path to our accomplishments? Or will our strength diminish, and tire us out? That all depends on yourself. You don't have to worry about monthly membership payments when it comes to getting yourself mentally stronger. Sweat out the small stuff and replenish with greater things life has to offer.

As Eleanor Roosevelt once said, "*You gain strength, courage, and confidence by every experience in which you really stop to look fear in the face. You are able to say to yourself, 'I lived through this horror. I can take the next thing that comes along.'*"

Unwanted Interruptions

December 14, 2018:

"Of all the things you choose in life, you don't get to choose what your nightmares are. You don't pick them; they pick you." –
John Irving

It's been a week since I've been here in Unit 6. I will say, the bed is *much* more comfortable than what I had to deal with in Unit 2, which was nothing. In here I had a mattress, a blanket, a pillow, and sheets. All the necessary tools for getting a good night's rest. As much as I am comfortable sleeping in a real bed, I still couldn't sleep. My sleep continues to be interrupted by bizarre nightmares. Some of them feel real. They all relate to each other over the same subject matter, which is ending my life due to depression.

Although some of the scenarios are a little ridiculous, they still end with the same result. These results are similar; in which they always wake me up in the middle of the night. After I gather my thoughts and feelings from the unexpected wake up call, I have difficulty falling back to sleep.

The nightmares are only temporary, for they do not remain in my thoughts the following day. New nightmares are created the following night, clouding my conscience with hatred. I don't think the nightmares will ever go away.

It's worse to realize you have no control over them. They just happen. In the end, they're not real. Still, they terrorize me during a time where I am expected to be relaxed and restful. If it continues, and at a more frequent rate, sleep will then become my enemy.

As sleep continues to bother me, so does my appetite. Depression can take a big toll on your eating habits and diet. Binge eating, portion control, unhealthy food choices. They all play a part in damaging your health and wellbeing. Can it be controlled? Absolutely. With the right approach to staying healthy, it can still take a lot of patience and determination.

The body figure we see every day in the mirror shows us the progress. A reflection never lies when you look straight at it. The image you see represents your true self. But it can be altered into a more positive image. The body can certainly change, but the face will always stay the same.

I worry too much about eating and sleeping, the two most important things to live a healthy, sustainable life. The balance between the two are off. When that happens, and that goes for anyone, your whole mental well-being can be thrown off. I used to think that sleep and appetite never affected my depression, but they did.

It was the lack of both that pushed my depression to higher levels. Depression then eliminated my sleep and appetite altogether. The power of depression can eventually eliminate our needs to survive. Sabotaging our health physically plays a major role in corrupting our mental health. And we need our mental health to keep on surviving.

December 18, 2017:

It was a loud crack, followed by a shout of pain. I was playing a basketball game that evening with some other inmates from my unit. As I jumped up to block a layup, I felt the basketball slam into my left hand, and jam my ring finger. The shout I made was short, as the injury happened so quick. Shortly after, the pain was gone, which I was surprised about considering how hard the impact of the injury was.

I continued to play, when suddenly my left hand started to become numb. After shaking my hand, I gained back feeling in my hand and continued to play on. A minute later, it was numb again. Again, I shook my hand aggressively and continued to play. I repeatedly had to perform this routine several times throughout the game. This was when I started to panic. I knew something was wrong, and I immediately went to the medical clinic.

On my way to the clinic, my ring finger became stiff. As I tried to bend it, I felt sharp pain run through my hand, as if someone stabbed it with a knife. This was more than just a jammed finger. The doctor examined my finger, and I noticed just then that my finger was as blue as a blueberry.

I was told by the doctor that it was fractured, just from his experience with broken fingers, although he was not an orthopedist. I would need an x-ray the following day and tape my last two fingers together to stabilize it. The doctor stated that the healing process would take about six to eight weeks. This news became more of a problem and discomfort for me, for I was left-handed. Even worse, there may be a chance I could not continue to write this book for the next month. Whatever it takes, no matter how little or slow I write, I will get it done.

<u>Season's Greetings</u>

December 25, 2017:

"Christmas is a season not only of rejoicing but of reflection." – Winston Churchill

It's Christmas Day. A holiday in here that depresses many patients. They struggle throughout the day, thinking about their families and loved ones. The hospital attempts to make everyone cheerful during the holiday, but it's not much.

Several days before Christmas, a holiday party is held in the gymnasium for all units. Tables are set up in rows, with red and green plastic tablecloths. Little pop-up snowman ornaments are placed on every table, while the gymnasium has holiday decorations taped along the walls. A DJ is blasting music from the stage, in front of an open space for patients to dance, if they choose to make fools of themselves in front of everyone.

Meanwhile, food is handed out. Food catered from a local restaurant. Two meatballs, macaroni and potato salad, two chicken tenders with honey mustard and ketchup, and a holiday cupcake to top off the holiday spirit. Soda is served as the beverage for this holiday feast, of course with no caffeine due to the caffeine-free policy in the hospital. Alcohol would have been nice, being a holiday and all, but it could've been worse with it. As the staff hands out the food, wearing ugly Christmas sweaters and decorated Santa hats, they briefly wish each patient a happy holiday.

At the end of the party, everyone is given a bottle of body wash as a small gift. In my opinion, I think it's more of a necessity for a lot of the patients. Their hygiene is very poor, filling the air with bad odors and a stench so terrible it makes you gag as you try to breathe. The body wash was a wakeup call, stating the obvious reason for the choice of gift.

On Christmas Day, we are treated with more holiday spirit. In the morning, gift bags are given to every patient. Inside the wrapped bags are a package of Oreos, a small bag of potato chips, peppermints, a bottle of skin lotion, a new pair of white socks, and a receipt for a $5 deposit in our bank account during our time here in the hospital. Nothing much, but it's the thought that counts. I'm shocked that the staff would be so thoughtful and generous to some of the monsters that live here.

The lunch for the day is another so-called "holiday meal". Rubbery prime rib, a baked potato with sour cream, green string beans, and a small slice of cheesecake stuffed into a Styrofoam cup. The evening snack later was a small cup of eggnog and some holiday cookies.

It seems that the theme for receiving holiday food and gifts is "small portions". Small enough to only last a few minutes with feelings of joy, misery to follow afterwards. All these Christmas treats received, when combined in total, is still more than what many patients here are given when not in prison. There's nothing more the staff can do to brighten the holiday spirit for everyone, except saying "Merry Christmas".

December 31, 2017:

"Be at war with your vices, at peace with your neighbors, and let every new year find you a better man." – Benjamin Franklin

New Year's Eve. It's a night in which I have been miserable on for the past few years. I would spend the evening celebrating by myself at home, stuck behind a TV and plopped on the couch. There wasn't any party to celebrate at, for my friends had been busy and distant.

Going out to some crowded bar by myself would be more miserable, for I would be in the middle of hundreds of drunk, joyous people having another memorable celebration with their friends. But celebrating in prison is even more depressing.

Not only am I by myself again, but I also reflect on the horrible year I just had, and where it has currently sent me in my crumbling life. Celebrating in prison was not considered celebrating. The prisoners were sent to their cells to lock in for the night three hours before the ball in Time's Square dropped. The guards were complaining about having to work throughout the night, instead of going out and getting drunk.

Most of the evening I spent watching TV with everyone else. It was too early for any of the New Year's Eve countdown shows to be on, so it was a night of edited movies on several cable channels.

The night dragged on and was quiet, as every prisoner thought to themselves. What will the next year be like? Will it be the year I finally get released, or just another wasted year spent here to punish me more?

Some of the other inmates who have been here for so long pay no attention to time. All they think about is getting older, missing the opportunities to turn their life around. Time is all you have when you're in prison for so long. It seems that holidays around here make everyone angrier and more violent.

While lounging on the couches, my friend Joe and I are watching TV, minding our own business from everyone else. At least, that's what I thought. Another inmate slowly approaches and gives us a blank stare. His eyes were more directed towards Joe. I could sense already that this was trouble.

As I averted my eyes back to the TV, Joe slowly got up from his seat and walked away towards his cell. He was followed by this suspicious, and perhaps dangerous inmate. Joe entered his cell and turned around to close the door, where the inmate was suddenly standing in the middle of his doorway.

They angrily stared at each other for about thirty seconds, not saying a single word. There they were, like statues, expecting something to happen. I strongly sensed a fight to break out between them instantly. My senses were right.

An explosion of fists erupted. There was more pushing and shoving than punches thrown. Most of the punches thrown missed their target due to the frantic and sporadic movement by both. The guards immediately broke up the fight. Joe and his opponent were locked in their rooms for the rest of the night.

While the other prisoner barely had a scratch on him, Joe was the complete opposite, and I mean that literally. Joe's face was covered with dark red, bleeding scratches. There must have been at least twenty scratches, and some were deeper through the skin and constantly bleeding. His face looked as if an army of cats attacked him. In this case, it was just one. Joe's enemy had long fingernails and found it more effective to use them rather than his fists. Afterwards, everyone else on the unit had to lock in early due to the fight. Four hours later, it was the year 2018.

January 1, 2018:

"All of us every single year, we're a different person. I don't think we're the same person all our lives." – Steven Spielberg

New Year's Day. It was 2018, and I started the new year by waking up, walking towards the showers, and suddenly approached Joe and his bandaged face. I asked him how he was feeling, and he responded that he was better. I didn't know if that was regarding his mood or his face. From the look of white bandages almost covering his entire face, I assumed he felt better and even more pissed off.

The day went on normal just like any other day. Rehab classes were cancelled due to the holiday. The guards walked in looking like they were up all night and still drunk, as they slowly dragged themselves to the couches and passed out for several minutes. With an entire day of lounging around and watching TV, it was not how I expected to spend the start of the new year, just when I thought about it how I would spend it over a month ago.

After dinner, considered to be the evening snack, everyone was given McDonald's to celebrate the holiday. If I was home, I would most likely go out for dinner at a nice restaurant, maybe order a filet mignon along with a nice bottle of red wine. Instead, I had two flattened cheeseburgers, as if someone sat on them, and a stale apple pie as hard as a brick.

As the day ended, I promised myself I would never have another New Year's Day like I did today. The journey of a great year begins with a single day that is even greater.

Hey Joe, What Do You Know?

January 14, 2018:

"You shall not steal, nor deal falsely, nor lie to one another." - Moses

It was gone. All of it. As I returned to my cell after my contact visit with my father, I noticed all my food and toiletries were stolen. I kept them under my bed inside the metal storage spaces. Most of the time I drape my blanket over to the side to cover up my items. But that didn't matter.

What mattered, was that I never locked the door to my cell. I usually leave my cell unlocked because theft is something that rarely occurs here in Unit 6. During my time here so far, I haven't witnessed anyone robbed of their personal items, even when they always kept their doors open. Today, I was the victim.

Since I got along with everyone in my unit, this theft was never expected to happen to me. Someone had to have been so desperate for food and hygiene products, that they went through any extreme circumstance to fulfill their hunger. As for the toiletries, it made me more annoyed than losing the food. They were items I needed daily, and ones that were not so cheap to purchase at the store.

I would have to wait three days until I visited the store again to replace the stolen items. More money to spend in my tight budget made me angry, for I wouldn't know what I needed soon to buy. Until I had money put into my account again, all I could do was wait.

I told the guards what happened, and all they could do was fill out an incident report, and hand it in to their supervisors. They would check the security cameras, which there are several located around the unit, and find out who the thief was. Even if they checked, and found out who it was, they still would not tell me. They would not reimburse me for any of the stolen items.

I was pacing, pondering all day trying to crack the case myself with the already given facts about my ward mates. I thought as hard as I could, but I was still stumped on finding out who it was. Before I went to bed that night, a guard knocked on my cell door and opened it. He came to tell me who the burglar was, for he also viewed the surveillance tapes of the incident. I felt shock run through my body when he told me. It was Joe.

January 19, 2018:

"Victory is always possible for the person who refuses to stop fighting." – Napoleon Hill

"Here we go again." That's exactly what I thought in my head when I saw my buddy Joe get into another fight. It was a fight he didn't start, again, but tempted his opponent like he always does. This matchup took place in the gymnasium while everyone was waiting to walk back to the units. The fight was about what all fights in this prison were usually about…nothing.

Another patient from our unit, Unit 6, was involved. Someone who Joe had a heavy grudge against during his time here. After this rival of his instigated Joe to finally fight him, it was time for the match we'd all been waiting for. As I predicted it to be a pushing scuffle, then leading to the submission of both on the floor holding onto each other, it turned into a serious boxing match. My prediction was wrong, and the results were unexpected.

It looked as if they were fighting for their lives, as there were periodic moments where the two would bounce around, with fists slowly stirring in front of their faces, and heavy breathing as if this was the final time they were able to breathe before dying. In the blink of an eye, Joe was struck in his left eye. A second later, another quick jab, this time in his right eye. Joe immediately collapsed backwards onto the hard, cold gym floor.

Before any more damage could be done, ten guards sprinted from the other side of the gymnasium and separated the two of them, instantly stopping the fight. One of the guards dropped their full cup of hot coffee, which splattered all over the floor, as he was the first to start sprinting and stopping the fight. I had never seen such a gruesome fight before, in person that is. And I was frightened, because I was right in front of them witnessing the entire fight.

An hour later, Joe returned to our unit. I could tell he was a mess, both physically and mentally. His right eye was covered with black and blue bruises. The left eye, which took the most damage, was completely shut, covered with larger bruises than the other eye. In addition, a deep gash was underneath his collapsed eyelid, with blood dripping down to his chin.

Joe was angry for what happened to him. He was disappointed in himself, losing another fight to add onto his winless record as a fighter. The nurse informed him he would need surgery, for his cheek bone was slightly fractured. She mentioned that the recovery time would be three months for the eye to fully heal. It's scary, to be told that your eye was almost lost, because it was borderline from losing its sight forever.

But Joe wasn't scared at all. He had a lot of heart and took the results of the fight rather well. It seemed like he brushed away this terrible news, as if he's been through it before. His nemesis would be locked in his cell for three days as punishment. That's it. A measly three days for an action that almost made someone blind.

Punishment is not taken seriously in this prison, and the staff doesn't care what happens between patients. It's very rare for justice to be served here for those who seek it, because they're already criminals.

In the meantime, Joe would always keep his distance from his enemy and stay cautious.

As for getting into more fights, he would most likely continue to do so just by looking at his past records of numerous altercations. Joe swore to himself that this would never happen to him ever again. The next three months would be spent staring down this patient with his one eye, filled with anger and furiously sharp, as he would wait patiently for the right time to seek revenge.

My Left Hand

January 22, 2018:

"Healing is a matter of time, but it is sometimes also a matter of opportunity." - Hippocates

I felt an immense amount of joy and relief, and it wasn't just from my heart. These feelings ran through my healed finger with such a bright energy, telling me that my hand was usable again. That means more writing, for this book at least, and other everyday functions which required immediate attention from my left hand. No more pieces of white, sticky bandage tape strapped to my fingers. And lastly, no more people asking me every day what happened to my finger.

When I heard the great news from the doctor, I was also told that the finger was still tender in terms of the healing process. I knew immediately what he meant when I couldn't fully fold my fingers into my hand as I made a fist. The level of pain was very low, and I was very close to having my finger rejoin the other fingers in complete dexterity. Just by staring at my finger and its slight deformity, the healing process was not complete.

It would be several months until it is set back into its right position, as it was before I had this misfortunate accident. The sides of my bottom knuckle were still red. I hope with future treatment, maybe physical hand therapy, this will not be permanent for the rest of my life.

Writing was the one concern I truly cared about, for I can express myself, and my emotions, through words I choose to share with others, as they read more of what I experienced during this traumatic time. Typing would not be a problem, no matter what the outcome of my finger was. I enjoy typing away on my laptop at such speed and accuracy. But it is the slow process of writing my words carefully, without automatic grammar and spell checks, that has more value and purpose.

Getting Older with Disappointment

February 8, 2018:

"Let us never know what old age is. Let us know the happiness time brings, not count the years." – Ausonius

Today is my birthday. I'm 33 years old, and I haven't even found the meaning of my life. I still await the significant moments to come, the ones in which I have made a major success both personally and professionally. I hadn't done anything to celebrate my past several birthdays. They were mostly spent at home, alone and depressing because of the absence of friends.

My 30th birthday, a milestone I hoped to be special, was a complete fail. I spent the day with a woman, who I was dating at the time. This day officially marked our third date together, and I chose to spend this special day with her. She insisted on this idea, which told me this woman could be "the one".

I went along with it not only because I liked her, but because I had no one else to celebrate the occasion with. The day consisted of a horrible movie we went to see, followed by a nice dinner with drinks at a restaurant out on the pier next to the Hudson River, overlooking a beautiful view of New York City at night.

And for my gift? A long text I received the following day from her, telling me she wasn't interested in seeing me anymore. I felt used, disappointed, and heartbroken knowing that my birthday was nothing but fake. She obviously felt sorry about me celebrating my birthday alone. After an important birthday milestone, I ended up depressed and isolated again. Some birthday.

As for today's birthday, it was still bad. I had to spend an entire day in prison, where there isn't any celebrating. No cake, no gifts, nothing. Instead I had three horrible meals throughout the day, which I barely ate, and a bottle of water. It was pathetic. I felt pathetic, and ashamed of myself for being stuck in this situation.

When other inmates had a birthday, they felt completely empty. Some of them would forget their birthday, for they knew getting older didn't matter anymore. They didn't have a life worth continuing, or celebrating, knowing that they lost everything. On a good note, I did receive birthday wishes from family and friends back home. But it wasn't the same. Several phone calls during the evening made it a little better, but not enough.

I also received some birthday cards through the mail. It did make me feel better, knowing that I was still thought of by others, kind enough to take the time to mail me something to commemorate the day. When the guard brought them to me, he tore open the envelopes and ripped open the cards and their multiple layers, making sure nothing was hidden inside of them. Afterwards, the guard would read the cards, all the personal writings intended for my eyes only, and finally slipped them under the door to my cell.

I just couldn't get a break today, a day in which I really needed one. Instead, I had another birthday wash out my happiness, and go down the drain into nowhere. Happy Birthday, Jared. Make your wish, and hope you get out of here soon.

February 14, 2018:

"We must accept finite disappointment, but never lose infinite hope." – Martin Luther King, Jr.

It's been nine weeks since I was first admitted to this psychiatric prison, and today I hoped my time here would end. I had my court hearing with the in-house judge, who would make the decision of my discharge. From what I was told when I was first admitted here, the process of being evaluated takes 60 days. It's been a little more than 60 days, but I was ready to leave no matter what.

Today is Valentine's Day. A day of love for those who share it with a special someone. I was hoping I'd be given some love from the judge in ruling of my discharge. And no, I don't mean *real* love, just some compassion and generosity towards my case. But it didn't happen. The judge ruled that I stay another 60 days, leading to another court hearing determining my discharge.

On a day where hearts were meant to be embraced, mine was broken. I barely got through the first 60 days here, and now this? But what can I do? Nothing. And now I'm here for another two months, where I would still be in danger of other criminals and something horrible could happen to me. I was frightened, worried, and most of all...disappointed.

Later that night, I reflected on the decision I received from the judge. This was unexpected, where I thought this entire time I was progressing so well, ready to move on. Maybe 60 days was not enough for me to overcome some of the biggest obstacles I'm dealing with.

My illness has created many problems in my life. One predicament after another is what makes the time pass by. Year after year, month after month, day after day. But it only takes a matter of seconds for my life to change. It will always veer towards positive or negative aspects of my life. For me, lately, it has pointed in the direction of failure and disappointment.

The time passes by slowly in prison when you're under tremendous stress. Your mind is consumed with racing thoughts and worries. They occur without any choices, and the control is lacking beneath the conscience. If one thought was to misfire, the action itself can take a serious toll. It can alter one's fate into a scenario they never thought they would be involved in. And at times, it can go too far. Unfortunately, I let one of my actions get the worst of me. The consequences are still pending.

What we do in life, stays with us until the end of our time. We never forget anything that occurs in our lives. In some memory, shape or form, it lives with us forever. And what I mean by "forever", is the remaining time for our lives individually. Memories may come and go, but they are not lost. They linger inside our heads, in our minds. When the moment comes for them to reappear, then they will benefit and remind us of who we truly are as an individual, and what we have done to make it so.

How can we make up for our past? What actions and tasks need to be conducted for the future? We are responsible for what happens to us. Whatever the outcome may be, we tolerate it. These actions are pressed into the mind and soul, they stay permanent, and they show how we came to be.

The past is the past. It has already been done. It can't be undone. I have trouble letting go of my past. I dwell on it too much, for it eventually gets me into trouble. Letting go has been complicated, and it continues, because it is all I have been living on.

Go Directly to Jail, Do Not Pass Go

March 12, 2018:

"Life is like riding a bicycle. To keep your balance, you must keep moving." – Albert Einstein

After I returned from my morning rehab classes, it was the usual time for me to be locked in my cell. It was Monday, the beginning of the week for the doctors here, and at this time they would come to my cell to do rounds and check on me. There was a loud bang on my door, and a guard entered the room.

For some reason when it comes to prison life, a loud knock on the door signifies trouble or an unexpected announcement that you are scared about. In this case, the guard told me it was time to go. At first, I didn't know what he meant.

Go where? No specific point of destination? I was confused and startled.

As I came out of my cell, he put his hand on my shoulder and told me I was leaving this horrid place. Finally, and for good. I had been waiting for this moment for four and a half months. I was rushed out of the unit, if someone was waiting for me to take me to my next destination on this traumatic journey.

I was leaving the unit, and I saw two guards go into my cell, throwing all my clothes and belongings into large garbage bags. My clothes from home, my stacks of books which kept me busy and productive, my notebooks, even this book you are reading right now. I guess that's how they pack around here.

I exited the facility, and I was greeted by the same officers that escorted me here several months ago in the ambulance. I was told that I was headed back home, but this time to county jail. This time around, during this next transition, I was excited and relieved.

I knew this meant that the process of getting me home was progressing. I assumed I would be in county jail for maybe a few days at the most, considering I have a private lawyer and my case would be moved up the list to be dismissed. But let's not get ahead of ourselves.

I entered the unmarked police car, placed in the backseat, and went onward to my next temporary living environment. I will say, this transport was much better than being strapped in an ambulance. With only my hands handcuffed, I enjoyed sitting upright in the backseat, comfortable as I stared out into the world through the window for the first time in almost five months.

After a fast, one-hour drive, I arrived at my next destination: county jail. This was the one stop in my journey to freedom that I had been dreading for the past five months. And yet, this day finally arrived.

As I was taken out of the car, escorted into the building, I was scared. I had the same fear as I did when I arrived at the psychiatric prison five months ago. But as I entered the building, and waited through a stressful, and painful process of checking in, I was scared even more.

It took over two hours of waiting around in a locked cell, taking my fingerprints, handing in all my clothing and belongings, and filling out paperwork. I was hurried at moments, and at other times stalled due to the long line of other incoming inmates, some returning criminals that were welcomed with open arms. I wasn't welcomed at all with such pleasant, sarcastic greetings.

Instead, I was bullied and ridiculed for my polite behavior, a character trait and manner unknown of here. And it was my politeness that made the officers question me and give me a harder time through this already difficult process. I was being called names, treated poorly because of their assumption that this was my first time I jail.

The worst part was when they were screening my body for scars and tattoos, as well as making me expose my private parts of my body. Before this step, when I told them I had no tattoos, they thought I was lying. A criminal coming into county jail, with no tattoos? That's a lie, and an insult to the officer's intelligence. But it wasn't. It was the truth, because in my heart I still believed I was not a criminal.

As for the scars, I had a few from past surgeries. I bet the officers thought they were stab wounds from a fight, or from some form of criminal activity. But as I stressed over and over to them again, they weren't.

When the screening process finally ended, I was escorted to where I would hopefully be stuck for the next two days only. Would I be thrown into general population, where the risk of getting beat up or killed is high? Or would I have my own cell, isolating myself from all the negativity this place has to offer.

The fear grew stronger inside my heart and stomach. The probability of having the worst experience here was high, and I was not ready for it. Not at all. As I carried my plastic, beaten mattress, probably holding the record for the most bedbugs inside of it,

I arrived at the place I was worrying about for the past few hours. The sign outside of the unit said, "Mental Ward", and seeing this gave me some sort of relief. How bad could this unit be? A mental unit? Everyone was probably so doped up on medication that they didn't even know where they currently were being held captive.

The door opened, and I was shoved into a small, crowded room. I stood there for a minute, confused and scared. I didn't know what to do next. Where do I put my mattress and toiletry bag? Do I start greeting other inmates?

To my surprise, several inmates approached me and greeted me. They even offered to take my stuff to an area where I would be staying. I was shocked and confused. Was I in the right place? This was county jail, right? As I met these dangerous individuals, I was given a tour of the small, crowded unit.

The first thing I noticed that bothered me was that the unit was very overcrowded with inmates, realizing that the officers had nowhere else to throw these degenerates to rot. There were rows of bunk beds. I counted sixteen beds total, yet twenty-seven inmates. Yes, the math does not add up.

My living area for these next two days would be on the floor. A dirty, disgusting, probably never cleaned floor. This is going to suck, I thought to myself. There wasn't even enough room on the floor to house the remaining inmates without a bunk bed.

To the left of the bunk beds, as I was shown on my brief and uninformative tour, were two small metal picnic tables. It was considered the lounge area, and the eating area, of the unit. My mattress and I ended up underneath one of the tables, for there was nowhere else to go. Underneath a table? You've got to be kidding me. I now truly felt like I was trapped inside a cage.

I threw my stuff down, and I was so tired and exhausted that I just wanted to lay down and sleep for the rest of the day. But I didn't want to, considering I was underneath a table. Dinner was soon, and I didn't want to have food drop all over me. So, I had no choice but to walk around and discover more of this hellhole.

As I carefully stepped over mattresses, with inmates lying on them, I made my way towards the end of the room which was where the bathroom was located. It wasn't even a bathroom, for it was not designated as a "separate" room. It was more like a wing of the room, like one of a studio apartment. But this was no studio apartment. This was hell all over again in a different shape and form, and I was living in it.

I approached the toilets and saw two metallic seats with a hole. That's it. Looks like I was going to be using a lot of toilet paper to cover these cold, disease-infested seats to sit on. There was no barrier or wall to cover this area for privacy. Just when things couldn't get worse.

Next to the toilets were two sinks, which look more like water fountains. And next to the sinks, a concrete hole in the wall that was considered the shower. It looked like a small cave and had a garden hose hanging at the top. And continuing with the lack of privacy theme for this area, the entrance of the shower was half covered with a clear garbage bag.

After my walkthrough of the bathroom area, I knew immediately that taking care of my hygiene here was going to be very difficult. And since it was only going to be two days spent here, from what my lawyer told me, I probably wouldn't even take care of my hygiene at all with these given conditions.

Above the row of bunk beds were two small TVs. At least there was some form of entertainment and tool of passing the slow time by. And what was better, was that there were two instead of one, offering less of a chance for fighting over which channel should be on. There weren't even remotes for the TVs, as I had to climb up onto someone else's bed to change the channel manually, which I found uncomfortable and annoying enough.

Along the entire left side of the ward was a wall of jail bars. Behind it, an officer sitting at a desk. Because this was a mental health unit, and there were risks of inmates harming themselves and others, an officer would be on 24-hour watch.

Yes, that's right. An officer would always be on duty to watch you sleep, eat, shower, go to the bathroom, and do whatever else you choose to do with your time stuck in here. Privacy was unheard of here, and that was just what I needed in this time of crisis.

March 13, 2018:

"No act of kindness, no matter how small, is ever wasted." - Aesop

I survived my first night here in this shithole, which was what I called it now as things got worse. Yes, it graduated from the term "hellhole". I was away at court during most of the day, and as I came back to the unit from my trip, I arrived with bad news. It seemed my case was going to be delayed, and the two days promised to me of staying in county jail was going to be broken. Instead of two days, I was informed of my stay here being extended for another two weeks.

Two weeks? How was I going to make it through this? How much more can I struggle with sleep? How much longer can I go without food and water before my body gives out? I chose not to eat any of the disgusting food, if it was even considered human food, and not even hydrate myself at least with the undrinkable water that was the only source available. I knew the next two weeks were going to be difficult, and one of the biggest challenges of my life.

The day surprisingly improved as one of the inmates helped me after I returned from court. I told him of my staying here for the next two weeks, and he felt sorry for me. The reason he felt sorry for me was because he knew this was my first time here in jail, and I was such an individual that did not belong here.

I showed him my bed location and the unbearable situation, and he immediately took my mattress. He dragged it towards a bunk bed at the end of the room, where he was sleeping on the top bunk, and threw it on the empty bedframe on the bottom bunk. Inmates in this unit would leave from time to time, being released I'm assuming or transferred elsewhere, and I knew a waiting list of inmates staying here before me were waiting for a bed to be vacant.

But this generous inmate, who seemed to oversee this unit and have authoritative role in this small community, let me cut the waiting list. I didn't know why he was being so generous to me, as I have barely had any conversation with him. I didn't even know his name. I was happy, shocked, surprised, and relieved.

There was no more sleeping on the dirty floor. Instead, I upgraded to a dirty, bottom bunk bed. I even had a great view of one of the TVs, as I could spend my days here lying on my hard, plastic mattress and watch TV. My day had gone from horrible, to somewhat hopeful. Now hope is what I need to survive in here.

March 27, 2018:

"No tendency is quite so strong in human nature as the desire to lay down rules of conduct for other people." – William Howard Taft

Two weeks have gone by. It is getting harder for me to fight through this environment and slow time that passes by in here. I spend most of my days sleeping, since I am getting weaker from not eating or drinking. I've showered only once since I've been here, and I've barely gone to the bathroom due to the lack of eating and drinking. My body was getting thinner, my face white and pale, and at times I had trouble walking around out of bed, lacking energy and risking my chance of falling and passing out.

Some of the other inmates were getting concerned. They were worried, thinking that this act of starvation was a way to end my life at such a slow pace. I gave them my meals, which they were extremely grateful for, yet confused about my eating habits here. The food didn't even look like food. It looked more like dog food if you ask me. And it probably was. That's what you get when you're in a real jail, and not some psychiatric hospital jail with decent food.

Most of the other inmates would devour the food every time it arrived, as if they hadn't eaten in weeks. They took whatever means necessary to survive in here, like their survival out on the streets. The schedule for meals was ridiculous, at least for breakfast it was. Breakfast was served at 4:30 in the morning. 4:30? That's absurd. My grandmother doesn't even eat breakfast that early. In fact, she's probably not even awake yet. But as my usual routine went, I gave away my breakfast tray and went right back to sleep.

As I try to get used to the routine of things here, I find some aspects of living in jail difficult. It seems that at any time, officers can order you to do anything they want when it came to protocol. One routine that occurred frequently throughout every day was something called "roll call", which was when the officer on duty would call out a list of names to see who was present. This would occur once every hour, and I mean every hour. That's right, even during the middle of the night when everyone is sleeping.

When roll call is announced, everyone is required to get out of bed, or stop whatever it is they're doing, and walk up to the officer giving your name. For a quick two-second process, it was annoying enough to interrupt you every hour, knowing that you couldn't even go anywhere else. But it was protocol, and it had to be done. As to why it was necessary during the middle of the night was crazy. There was no way to escape, not even enough room to do so. Maybe conducting these "roll calls" was punishment or torture, and probably both.

Another routine that happened every few days was "tossing the cells". Most of the time this occurred was in the middle of the night. This process was when several officers would raid the unit, kick all the inmates out, and spend over an hour tearing the unit apart. That meant going through everyone's toiletry bags, beds, and every other exposed space throughout the unit. They conducted this to check for contraband and weapons. Meanwhile, I'm standing outside in the hallway lined up against the wall, with my hands up high on the wall, being frisked several times throughout the check.

Afterwards, when the process is complete, everyone is led back inside the unit to find the entire place wrecked. Mattresses would be tossed all over, as well as belongings. It takes about an hour just to clean up everything and figure out whose stuff belongs to who. I always thought tossing the cells was purposely conducted in the middle of the night for more torture. When the officers rush into the unit, banging and yelling for you to wake up, they approach and drag you out of your bed. It was madness. Everything I witnessed and went through here so far was madness. How much longer will I have to go through the madness, and will it get worse?

The Hunger Strike

April 2, 2018:

"The only way to keep your health is to eat what you don't want, drink what you don't like, and do what you'd rather not." – Mark Twain

I went to court again today, hoping for some good news. Instead, I found out my release would be delayed again for another two weeks. The judge was not convinced enough that I would be safe towards myself and others. I knew that I had been eager to continue with my life in a safe manner for weeks now, but the judge was biased against those with a mental illness. Although I cannot get into the details of my case, let it be known that things were progressing, but it would take some more time.

I was still not eating or drinking, and I grew weaker as each day passed. Other inmates were still worried about my health, and on a few occasions, I would be offered snacks or food. There was an online store available for an inmate to order "real" packaged food, or "commissary" as it is called. The delivery for commissary would come once a week, and many inmates who had money available would opt to purchase these food items. When you're in a small room with over twenty grown, hungry men, three small meals given in jail throughout the day is not enough. The food item ordered the most from commissary was ramen noodles. And that was the only thing desirable and worth eating in this awful place.

Now, I could only eat what was offered to me. This is the only way I could survive in here. In a few weeks, if I'm still here and I continue to starve myself, my health may be at risk. But starvation was a necessity for me in this place, and hopefully a temporary one. In a dangerous place like the one I'm living in right now, food will not be the only thing to help me survive.

April 3, 2018:

"Bad food is made without pride, by cooks who have no pride, and no love.

Bad food is made by chefs who are indifferent, or who are trying to be everything to everybody, who are trying to please everyone.

Bad food is fake food, food that shows fear and lack of confidence in people's ability to discern or to make decisions about their lives." – Anthony Bourdain

It took two weeks of finally getting money wired to my jail account from family members, and of course waiting a week for the food to arrive. But I finally had some decent food to eat, after starving myself since I first arrived here. As my food was delivered, I had all the other inmates swarming me, asking for some of my food to share. I didn't know how much longer I was going to be stuck in here, and I needed to ration my portions carefully to not fall back into starving again.

I was so hungry and weak, and extremely desperate to eat something. I could probably eat the entire supply of food in one sitting. I had to think smart, and not give up any of my food. My duty now was to protect my bag of food, already knowing that I barely had a spot to hide it. The only place I could hide the bag was under my mattress, hoping that my food wouldn't get squashed considering I laid in bed all day. The pestering and begging from the other inmates wouldn't stop. Sometimes I was afraid when I said "no" to them, risking getting them angry or upset, or expecting to have to give some legitimate reason why I chose not to share what was so precious to me.

The fear I had the most with protecting my food was for it to be stolen, just like what happened in the psychiatric jail. I had more food this time, but less space to hide it. There were moments today, only an hour after my food arrived, that others tried to sneakily steal my food without my looking. I was cautious, protective of a garbage bag full of food worth twenty-dollars. This bag of food was my lifeline to surviving in this place. No longer could I sacrifice my body and health with starvation.

In an environment where trying to kill yourself is impossible, because of the tight security and observation, it seemed I was becoming successful with my starvation method. The guards never noticed, or even cared. But the thing was, after all I've been through, and with such a transformation of finally thinking optimistically about my life, I didn't want to end up killing myself.

Some of the nicer inmates I became friendly with were asking me for my ramen noodles because they wanted me to partake in a ritual food cuisine popular in jail known as a "hook-up". So, what exactly is a "hook-up"? At first, as it is commonly used on the outside, I thought it was something sexual that I absolutely did not want to be involved in, and then I became scared. But it absolutely was not that.

A "hook-up" is when a large assortment of commissary items such as ramen noodles, crackers, meats, condiments, and other items to make it tolerable and not too disgusting, are mixed together. A large, clear garbage bag is used to store everything. Some inmates will chop up some of the ingredients with their hands in preparation, and some will fill the bag with hot water and ramen noodle packets to get things started. After all the ingredients are finally mixed in together, the large garbage bag is tossed around, which is also known as the "cooking" process.

The garbage bag is then opened, laid out flat on the table, and an enormous rectangle of the "hook-up" is set out. It looked like a birthday cake, as slices were handed out to inmates and thrown onto a slice of soggy bread. I never took part in any of the "hook-ups" during my time here. Just looking at the result, even the presentation of it, made me sick and nauseous.

At the same time, it was nice to see some sort of tradition and activity of togetherness between the inmates. The bonding through preparing a feast of disgust, and the collaboration of sharing such valuable food items, was strongly displayed. I watched them as they devoured the food, laughing and sharing stories. They even discussed about new ideas and suggestions for creating "hook-ups" in the future. It was like seeing a family come together for a holiday meal. And although I was not eating the main course of this feast, I was still part of the family.

Hate Thyself, Top Oneself

April 7, 2018:

"That's the thing about suicide. Try as you might to remember how a person lived his life, you always end up thinking about how he ended it." – Anderson Cooper

It's Saturday night, early evening, and majority of the inmates locked in my unit are headed off to a church service located in the jail's chapel. They would probably be gone for an hour or so. Some other inmates and I were left here to watch TV and relax, enjoying the open space and decrease of noise. It was quiet, relaxing, finally a night in which I didn't hear bickering and fighting between inmates and yelling across the room.

There was an absence of inmates walking around the tight space, lingering among others lying in their beds and watching TV. Maybe I could finally get some rest here for once. This certainly was my opportunity to do so, and with only sleeping an hour or two every night here, I took advantage of it.

As I'm lying on my bed, finally relaxing with some form of peace and calmness from the environment, a loud boom erupted next to my bed. I was startled, scared as I jumped up from my bed. It felt like my ears popped just from the loudness of the crash that occurred next to me. Before I could turn around and discover what it was, thoughts were racing through my head.

Did my bunk mate on top of my bunk bed fall out of bed by accident? Did someone drop something? Is there a fight going on? Was something loud on one of the TVs? I slowly turned my head towards where the sound came from. My thoughts were racing quicker as my head turned. And then I saw it. I saw…him.

My bunkmate who I'd known and become close with for the past few weeks was lying on the floor next to my bed. He in fact did fall out of his bed. I thought it was a joke at first, but it wasn't a joke at all. And then I thought, "How could someone actually fall out of their bed like that?" I went towards him lying on the cold, hard floor. He was laying on his stomach, with his head turned to the side. His eyes were closed, and his body was still. He wasn't breathing.

I sat up in my bed and repeatedly called his name, asking if he was okay. No answer. I called for help from the officer on duty and other inmates. The officer was aware of the situation, although he did not see it happen, and was already using the phone to call for medical assistance. As for the other inmates, they looked at me strangely and didn't answer to my cries for help. They just sat there, in their beds, and some even returned their eyes to the TV they were watching. I asked if any of them saw what happened. The only response I received was from one inmate nearby who stated, "I saw him jump."

I panicked and was shocked to hear what he said. No way could he have jumped on purpose like that. But he did. And then at that moment, I knew exactly what happened. He leaped from the top of his bed and dove head first into the ground. His goal was to somehow break his neck, leading to his death. It was a suicide attempt. Just when I thought this place was impossible to try and end your life, I was wrong.

As I realized what happened, I yelled out more for help, this time directed at the officer on duty. I quickly walked up to the guard behind the bars and pleaded for him to help. He couldn't come inside the unit to help me and check on my friend. Apparently, the officer on duty was not allowed to enter the unit if there was any sort of emergency, whether it be a fight or medical situation.

When this protocol was explained to me by the officer, I was confused and annoyed as I talked back at him. "What do you mean? I need your help! I think he's seriously hurt." The officer stood there, not responding to my pleas for help. After I ranted about him not helping, he still did not respond, and eventually went back to sit at his desk. This was absurd! This was madness! What kind of place is this?

I couldn't leave my friend lying there unattended, so I hurried back. I stood next to him and remained there until help arrived. There was nothing I could do at this moment except wait. I was afraid to move him the slightest bit, in case he was still alive and moving him might cause further injury.

I looked at my friend, his body lying on the cold floor, and then looked at the top of our bunkbed. I put the pieces of the puzzle together for this horrible accident and figured out that he jumped from the top of his bed to try and break his neck. He performed what some would call, a "swan dive", where one would dive head first with their arms spread open in a body of water. There was no body of water here. Instead, a body of hard, dirty concrete.

Ten minutes went by since I heard the body slam to the ground. Still no movement from my friend. His chest was still, and from the look of it he wasn't breathing. It was at that moment when I realized my friend might have been dead. There was a chance he was forever gone, no longer a part of this beautiful world despite his current situation. I didn't know what to do next. I continued to stand there, staring at his body on the floor.

As I stood there in shock, I felt waves of adrenaline flow through my body. I've seen people lying on the ground hurt before, but this instance gave me chills because it was a suicide attempt. With these frightening feelings I was experiencing at this moment, my body and mind remained calm. My hands and legs were steady, and my thoughts were blank.

Forty minutes passed by since he jumped and help finally arrived. I was still standing there like a statue. There were two officers and a nurse entering the unit with a stretcher. I couldn't move as they ordered me to move aside and let them do their job. I was in shock, and I didn't want to leave my friend. I eventually moved, standing nearby the scene.

The nurse and officers spent no more than a minute to check on my friend and made the conclusion that he was dead due to an act of suicide. The two officers picked him up from the ground, not even carefully, and threw him on the stretcher like a piece of meat. After they strapped him in, they started to roll the stretcher out of the unit. As they were leaving, one of the officers said to the other, "One less to worry about."

I couldn't believe it. Not at all. How could someone say something like that? Why did this officer make this statement, or comment, or whatever he considered it to be? As the door slammed shut after they exited, I remained standing still. I stood there for several minutes, with my head staring down at the ground. I just witnessed someone die right next to me, a suicide of all things, and saw three professionals take him out like nothing happened. They didn't even throw a sheet over his body in respect as they rolled him out on the stretcher. I saw my friend's lifeless body taken out of the unit.

I was traumatized by what I saw, and how it was handled. My reaction to this was confusing, as I couldn't even cry. I was stunned, helpless to myself and my friend. What pissed me off more, was that the other inmates didn't pay attention to the entire incident. If everyone else was back from their church service, more help would probably have been offered. But as they all were out, busy praying to God, one individual back here in the unit sent himself to God.

No one wants to know the exact time of their death. No one. Unfortunately, there are those who choose to set their date of death. These people are the ones who choose to take their own lives by committing suicide. It is one of the world's leading causes of death. It happens every single day. And what is the result? A victim is lost, and the individual is forever gone.

In the end, the real victims are those who are part of this individual's life. There is more harm brought onto others, rather than the victim. It's an unfortunate event that will stick with those closest to you until their own time has ended. It's a tragedy that is unbearable to live with. As for the word "committed", I still do not know why many use this term. Nothing has been committed. No crimes, no sins, no commitments. Just a helpless act by an individual, who needed help to begin with.

It was the first time I saw someone die right in front of me. My friend had more courage to do what I tried to do several times myself, which was commit suicide.

He succeeded, and he finally found a way out of this horrid place and life he was living.

There's a saying, or more like slang, used in British prisons describing those who decide to kill themselves: "top oneself". It can also be said as, "top yourself", which is more of the U.S. version of this slang phrase. This phrase may be not be said frequently, but it does occur. So do the suicides.

And so, I saw this man "top himself". This was a tragedy for me to experience. Yet, this was also a sign for me. I couldn't do what he did to himself. I didn't just need to survive. I needed to live.

April 8, 2018:

"If you're that depressed, reach out to someone. And remember, suicide is a permanent solution, to a temporary problem." – Robin Williams

I spent most of the day lying in my bed reflecting on what happened to my bunkmate last night. There's really nothing else to do in here but lie in bed and watch TV. But today was different, considering last night's event. I thought a lot about my attempts with suicide, which obviously I did not follow through with.

Suicide has been my biggest fear for the past several years. The ideations and thoughts about suicide corrupt my mind with negativity and hopelessness. It has been, for a long time, my defense mechanism against others during conflict, and the method of not treating a problem properly. This one powerful word, "suicide", has caused numerous problems, where instead I used it to avoid problems.

There have been several close calls when it came down to suicide attempts. Although there have been so many ideations of it running through my mind when depressed, I never had any set plan. I always assumed that I would never go through with it, and I didn't have anything to provoke me. But at times, when I'm in an extreme state of depression, there are tendencies that can go a little too far, but still at the point of prevention.

Taking an overdose of pills, there is the choice of swallowing or spitting them out. On a bridge, you are on the edge of either falling forwards to your death, or backwards onto safe ground. In a car, you can drive into oncoming traffic or continue driving on the correct side of the road. With all these scenarios, you are on the border between life and death. Each side you decide to take will stay with you forever, for life is precious and death is terminal. I have come to learn through these experiences that life is the side to stick with.

The time I make for myself after this right decision is what will persuade me to make my life memorable and precious to value forever. Making these decisions, as I see it, are permanent. Therefore, after learning through such traumatic experiences, I chose to permanently live out the rest of my life. I wish I had thought of this concept before these events happened, but I guess I had to learn the hard way, just to realize what the right way was. I regret having these episodes and ask myself daily, "Why couldn't I avoid any of it?"

The answer was simple: depression made me optimistic and hopeless, creating a comfort zone to live in when it is not comforting at all. To avoid conflict, I took the cowardly way out by saying harmful comments about myself. It made others uncomfortable and frightened, but I didn't feel the same way. I was used to it after a while, so much that I used it as an excuse for almost everything.

It was my way of getting out, escaping from anything that would interfere with my being happy. After a while, when the thoughts were built as high as a skyscraper, it would all come crashing down. Panic and fear would take over my body. The control of my negative thoughts was lost, and I hoped my positivity would retaliate and battle against this darkness.

The various suicide attempts, the suicidal ideations, all those trips to the hospital, and the immense amount of sabotage I brought onto myself. In the end of it all, and after each event was over, I was never defeated. Never. I'm still breathing, my heart continues beating, and I can see and feel the real person that I am. It is determined that taking the easy, yet permanent way out was not destiny.

If I could have such strength and courage to prevent suicide, making a life-threatening mistake, then I am destined to continue living a fulfilling life. And that's exactly what I need to do from now on. My conscience needs to feed off these positive traits I possess within myself and apply them consistently to avoid any future problems. I strongly fear if I will fall apart again when problems arise ahead of me. But now, I know that my fear has vanished.

It's strange how the world perceives depression, or any mental illness for that matter. Sensitive and unordinary topics, such as "suicide", makes others uncomfortable. Even the moment when it is first brought up, the moment when that powerful word "suicide" pops up and its pronunciation is clear into thin air, a force of fear emerges from the reaction of the other individual this word is targeted to. Eyes will open widely and roll to the side, a short gasp is projected without warning, a slight pause before an anticipated response, all occur within seconds of this awkward interaction.

But why does it have to be awkward? Why is "suicide" treated so sensitively as if it is ready to shatter, like thin glass? When will the time come that this topic, happening every day and all over the world, is treated and discussed without fear? Suicide continues to occur with those seeking a solution to end their pain and suffering, especially when in a mental state. The problem is not finding the right answers. It is finding the opportunities and resources for help.

Many seek to find satisfactory resolution for their problems, and many are unaware of the methods and support systems laid in place to help us as a society. Does everyone in need of help deserve it?

Absolutely. Should insurance or any issue with affordability interfere with this desire? Absolutely not. It should not matter what socioeconomic background you come from, or any other distinction that some consider prejudice, every single human being deserves to be educated and treated. And what if there was a way to share these valuable, lifesaving tools for everyone to access without any prerequisites or requirements? There should be. And one day…there will be.

Saving lives and preventing suicide should not have a cost attached to it. It is an opportunity to grasp at any available moment without hesitation and thought. This opportunity is vital to be a part of everyone's lives and a part of human nature. It needs to be as important and reliable, like a simple breath of air, such an action we use constantly to survive.

The question that comes into mind when "treatment" and "help" are suggested in one's recovery is, "Will it work?". Just by asking that question will signify a strong chance of it not working for yourself. You must strongly be assured that it is going to work. There is no set timetable of when things need to progress, and there are no limitations into how much effort and work is put in.

Accepting the fact that everything will work out is the first step to making it work. It's not worth stepping backwards for that one important step, when you already have your foot in the door leading to recovery. Once you've stepped inside, you are in. You may have times where your steps can wander off in circles, misleading you down the wrong path.

Eventually, whatever time it takes, you will find your way back. There's only a certain amount of space in our lives to get lost in, just like when we are lost geographically. If there was such a map to guide us in the right direction, then this map is our ultimate tool for leading us towards the right direction.

I believe that every single person battling with depression can be saved. And they deserve to be saved. No one asked for the depression to enter their life. It just happens, whether caused by events or not. Things can happen to us at any moment in our lives, and we cannot predict what will happen next. Staying optimistic about being aware that there *are* resources to help with depression, is just as important as finding these resources. And that goes for anyone, depression or not.

As a society, we need to be educated more and resourceful for those we care about struggling with depression. As human beings, we cannot depend on one individual to help many. Not only do we need to help ourselves with the strength within us, but we need strength and support from others.

My bunkmate was battling with his problems, and he lost. He took his own life, never knowing if there was any hope in getting better. What if he *was* receiving treatment and it wasn't enough to save him? What if he didn't receive treatment at all? There are many questions to this mystery I witnessed, and now I'll never know the answers.

It's hard to battle through depression on your own. If it was so easy, the world wouldn't have so many individuals *still* struggling with it. There wouldn't be as many resources in today's world to help us that we are grateful to have access to. We're lucky. We're stronger. And we need to take advantage of it.

"Superman may be unable to rescue every single person on Earth. But he can still save us all by giving hope." – Jared Penn

<u>Do You Mind?</u>

April 11, 2018:

"Be happy in the moment, that's enough. Each moment is all we need, not more." – Mother Teresa

Today I took the opportunity to go outside for some fresh air. It was the first time I had been outside in a month. During my time away so far, I have been through two seasons: Winter and Spring. The temperature outside changed over time. From the beginning of my journey when it was freezing cold, to today where it was warm and yet cool at times.

I was taken to the roof of the building, where I saw two blacktop courts. One was a basketball court, and the other a volleyball court. I was the only inmate outside for the next hour, and as lonely as it was, it was nice to get away from the overcrowded and noisy unit. Besides, I needed to feel what fresh air was like again, for I missed it terribly.

It was even hard at first breathing in the mild, cool air into my lungs. My chest would hurt at times, probably from the long absence of being outside. I had been stuck inside for a long time with moldy, dusty air surrounded by bad odor from the other inmates.

I decided to sit on the ground to the side of the basketball court, with my back against the wired fence. I looked around to check out my surroundings. There was barbwire all along the tops of the fences. Surveillance cameras were in every corner of the buildings around me. In a place like this, you're always being watched. In the distance, I saw the top half of several buildings.

One building, an old church, was in the center of my view. The church had to have been at least two-hundred years old from the look of it. It was dark, structured with old bricks and covered with marvelous statues. At first, I thought I was looking towards a beautiful, European city with wonderful church structures centuries old.

But I wasn't. I was in a poor, rundown city in New Jersey. Nothing special. But looking at this old church seemed special to me during my time out here, during this moment where I had the time to reflect on everything that has happened to me these past few months.

Not only did I stare at the old church, but I also admired the beautiful view of the sky. It was a clear, sunny day. Not a single cloud in the sky. I finally had the sun shining on my face, as I felt relaxed in this calm setting. I missed this feeling of warmth upon myself, and this feeling of temporarily being free from all the horror inside of the jail below me.

But my freedom isn't there yet. I still must wait. And as I sat there outside, I worried about how much longer that would be. There wasn't any time to continue worrying. My time needed to be spent focusing on getting out of here. During this hour, sitting outside by myself, was the only time here I had to focus.

The mind is always there, with you. If it is lost, then eventually it must be found. If it is broken, then the right treatment will repair it. It may be shattered into pieces if that's the case. Mental treatment, including medication, is the glue to put these pieces back together. Dig deep enough through these methods, and you will find it, of course, in one form or another. The mind will always remain as "the mind".

Whether it moves from one thought to another or uses tactics that are unorthodox compared to how the human mind should work, it will always be yours to keep. Taking care of our mind, is like taking care of a child. We have a duty as human beings to provide it with the right nutrients, so that eventually over time it has the capability to take care of us. And in doing so, our mind will function properly. That's what happens when it works for such a long time. As life goes on, there are moments where it starts to shut down unwillingly.

There is one major concept I learned during my recovery, and I still use it to this day. It's called "mindfulness". Sounds simple, right? Well, it's not. Practicing it doesn't make perfect, it makes permanent. Mindfulness helps us stay within the present, and not dwell so much on the past or future. It may be a psychological tool, but why can't any ordinary person use it? Well, many do not even realize they're using it. It's just natural. We focus on how we're currently living our lives. Am I hungry? Am I tired? How do I feel right now? What am I going to do right now?

If I were to tell someone that mindfulness works, would they believe me? Would they question whether it could work for themselves? It will work, if you use it right. Meditation, breathing exercises, whatever method is chosen, even if you have your own. Just know, anyone can have the capability to practice it. The availability of mindfulness will always be there.

Well, to prove to people that mindfulness *does* work, I used it a lot to help me get through my time away. My experience with mindfulness helped me with my writing. Otherwise, how else could I have come up with all that material? In fact, my time outside admiring the beautiful scenery in a negative environment, by myself, gave me an opportunity to practice mindfulness. No distractions among an almost perfect moment away from all the horror I must live with.

If anyone read my entire story and the success of using mindfulness, maybe they'd try it themselves. I say to you, the one currently reading this, "Go ahead. Try it. It doesn't hurt to try it. In fact, it feels good." When you realize you've used mindfulness successfully, I'll be the one inside your head saying, "I told you so."

Can't We All
Just Get Along?

April 13, 2018:

"We focus so much on our differences, and that is creating, I think, a lot of chaos and negativity and bullying in the world.

And I think if everybody focused on what we all have in common - which is - we all want to be happy." – Ellen DeGeneres

The unit had some inmates with unusual characteristics and behaviors. Some didn't seem like they were even in reality, as if they were in another dimension with themselves. The odd behaviors they exhibited explained clearly why they were placed in a mental health unit in the first place. And as for the other inmates, they were somewhat violent and irritated, yet remained calm the majority of my time here. Except for one person.

He was an angry individual, always complaining and yelling at other inmates for their insubordinate behaviors and manners. There is no such thing as manners when it came to county jail. At times, he would always explain how he had been in the prison system for a long time, knowing the correct mannerisms and tactics of how to survive such an environment. But I didn't need his advice or expertise on how to survive this place. My goal was to get out of here, and fast.

Some of the other inmates explained to him that such an individual as myself didn't need his advice. They told him I was intelligent, that I didn't belong here, that I had potential to continue with a normal, successful life. And this is exactly what angered him. He was jealous, envied my past, present, and future success to come. His anger suddenly erupted into yelling and cursing towards me.

As he started approaching me, with the intention of eventually attacking me physically, other inmates insisted that he immediately stop and prevent himself from getting into trouble. But now I saw why he was placed in the mental health unit. He had anger management issues, which would eventually turn into violence. And for someone that had committed murder before, I was not surprised.

He approached me with anger and intimidation. I expected the punches and kicks to pour onto me, and I was scared. Just as the first punch was thrown, another inmate I barely knew stepped in front of me. The punch landed on his face, but he remained standing in front, protecting me. I stood back several steps away from them both, and the punches continued to land on this random individual's head.

My savior, my protector, fell to the ground. Punches continued to blow towards his head, with blood gushing out from the side. Officers then came in and stopped the fight. The angry fighter was removed from the unit, restrained by several officers, yelling at everyone. As he left, I hurried to the hurt inmate on the ground. He was knocked out unconscious, and bleeding all over his head.

Before I could call for medical attention to help him, several more officers and nurses entered the unit. They carried him out immediately. After they left, I remained standing there next to scene of the fight. It wasn't much of a fight. It was more like a severe beating with no retaliation. I stood next to a small pool of blood, with a path of blood drops leading to the unit door.

Everything happened so quickly. The fight felt like an instant flash and left me quiver and tremor afterwards with fear. I didn't know what just happened. I was confused as to why some stranger I barely talked to would step in for me like that. Why would he take a beating so severe and sacrifice himself so far to almost lead him to his death? And why did he do it for me? I was shocked, and mostly surprised.

No one had ever rescued me before from such a massacre. At the same time, I felt honored. I felt like I was a king, and a noble knight just protected me from death. Maybe it was a sign telling me that I needed to keep on surviving in this place I call a dungeon. It was the nicest thing anyone had ever done for me, but it was also the scariest. I didn't know if I should be grateful for what he did for me, but I was grateful that I was still alive.

Hope Is A Good Thing

April 16, 2018:

"We have always held to the hope, the belief, the conviction that there is a better life, a better world, beyond the horizon." – Franklin D. Roosevelt

It's Monday, the beginning of another week here stuck in a dungeon full of prisoners. I didn't sleep at all throughout the night. Last night was busy in the "add more prisoners to our unit" department, as six new inmates moved in throughout the night one by one. It's unexpected when a new inmate will move into our unit, but I was always cautious because it could be any dangerous criminal. One who could cause further problems, or one who I could befriend.

In addition, there was barely any more room to fit another inmate. There were already nine people sleeping on the floor. Soon enough, I wouldn't have anywhere to walk. In the middle of these "new inductees" to our hall of shame, we also had officers wake us up and toss us out of the unit for contraband check. Thankfully I was already awake. But standing out in the hall, my arms up against the wall, and constantly being frisked was torture. I stood there for almost an hour, and half of the time I could barely keep my arms up. That's how tired I was.

As I try to start this new day, another day here in county jail, I have hope ahead of me. Tomorrow I have another court appearance. After all the trouble my family, lawyer, and doctors had to go through these past weeks trying to get me out of here, this would hopefully be the last time they'd all convince the judge to finally let me go home.

Everyone anticipates my release tomorrow, as do I. I couldn't spend another day in here. The starving from disgusting food and lack of sleep were wearing me down. I was worried about tomorrow, when I should be hopeful instead. It wasn't my court appearance that I was worried about, but it was about my future and what I was going to do with it.

I have seen some variations of a happy life ahead of me, as if I was moving closer towards a brightness of hope. There is an available source of ingredients, combined to make the right recipe to utilize. The light at the end of the tunnel, as I see it, should not signify the end of it all. Instead, it should represent the anticipation of a life filled with warmth and comfort.

It seems that my problems with life itself are the transitions of it. Whether it's from college to college, job to job, or one group of friends to another, the transitional phase seems to be a struggle I deal with. The reason can be due to my depression, but I strongly believe it's mainly focused on coping with it. There's always a fear of losing these valuable assets in my life, if my transitions aren't handled carefully. The risk is even greater when my depression gets in the way.

Planning the rest of your life can be simple, or in some cases difficult. Sure, many have an idea of how their life should turn out. Hard work, years of planning, sacrifices to make ends meet. But what happens when our planned timeline is interrupted? There are bumps down the road, a hiccup in your life, if you will.

Perfection is as scarce as exquisite riches many hope to obtain. If one were to have a "perfect" life, then how can you even call that a "life"? I think challenges and unexpected occurrences were meant to bring life up and down. The lessons we learn from our mistakes are what mold us into true human beings. Lessons in life are supposed to heal and educate us. You must learn how to walk first, before you can start running.

The mistakes we make cannot be undone. If there was a way to go back and prevent them, they would be erased and cease to exist. Unfortunately, that's not the case. We at times learn from our mistakes in a difficult manner. Does that mean the turnaround is even greater?

Once a mistake is fixed, it's fixed. There should not be a limit of time it is to be completed, or a scale to measure the effort. The lessons learned should be retained in our mind. Our storage capacity for these lessons should be infinite, allowing us to learn as much as we can to prevent them from ever happening again.

April 17, 2018:

"In three words I can sum up everything I've learned about life: it goes on." – Robert Frost

I went to court today…again. But this time, good news arrived for me. News that I had been waiting for the past several weeks here in county jail, and for the past several months in a psychiatric prison. It was six months since I had been arrested back at home, and from when my journey started. Today, it has finally come to an end. My journey to freedom has ended.

Due to the privacy of my case, I cannot discuss the details in how it ended. But the one fact, and the only fact I cared about, was going home. I was free from this world of degenerates and criminals, of a living environment intolerable for an individual of my background, in a confined place where authority treats you horribly and ridicules you. Too long have I been having trouble sleeping, having restless nights interrupted with nightmares. Too long have I spent more than half of my time starving myself. I can finally eat again, normal food that is, and I can finally get a good night's sleep.

There is something I will miss from my time away from home. They are the people I met that become friends. Some of them may never return home, that is, if they even have a home to go to. Some will eventually be released, but will they stay away from trouble and not return to prison?

I always wondered if I would ever run into anyone I've met these past six months away out in the real world. What would I say to them? Would they even recognize me? Would they still consider me a friend? I have this strong feeling that I probably won't see them ever again. We come from different neighborhoods, different socioeconomic backgrounds, a different form of society to blend in and dwell with. They will always stay in my mind and heart from time to come, for I know this journey I travelled on will never leave me.

I returned to my unit and started packing up my belongings. It wasn't much, considering I wasn't allowed to keep any personal belongings in jail. So, it was just me and my dirty, battered plastic mattress. As I dragged myself and my belongings to the door, I stood there waiting for my release to come.

I noticed that I still had some of my commissary left over from the week, and I didn't need to take it with me. I was going home to an endless supply of food of my choice. The commissary bag was in my hand, and I gave away the rest of my food. Inmates were running up to me, begging and pleading for me to give them something. It was as if I was giving away money, but unfortunately this was in the form of ramen noodles and saltine crackers.

The inmates I befriended came up to me and said their goodbyes. I even received a few hugs. I don't know why, considering we weren't as close. But to them, I was an empathetic inspiration to them. A kind-hearted, intelligent individual who saw them as human beings, and not as criminals. They were happy for me that I was finally going home. They didn't so much envy me for my leaving, but instead knew that I didn't belong here.

This was not where I needed to be right now. Right now, I needed to return home getting further treatment. I needed to attend an extensive out-patient program to learn the skills needed to cope with my depression. And I needed to receive the proper medication that will stabilize my feelings and thoughts. Most of all, I needed to rebuild my life through family, friends and my professional career. It was time to move on. And so, I did.

As much as this was the journey I did not ask for, I did learn something valuable. Part of life for everyone is trying to get past obstacles and challenges in your way. Some things we achieve in life are harder to grasp than others, and yet we have found that everything we want in life does not come easy. If that were so, then living would be much simpler.

We do what we can to satisfy ourselves to the fullest, and at the same time do what needs to be done for our individual needs. Living day to day, as if we were on autopilot, should not be ignored or tampered. Yet, some find at times that when our autopilot is switched off, and we're on manual, it's a heavier burden to carry when we already have so much in front of us to worry about. And that's just the problem right there.

Worrying about what's in front of us, what our future holds and how it will unfold. We can't assume what will happen to us, because our assumptions can deceive us and lead us to discomfort. The comfort won't be there because whatever happened wasn't expected or planned, and then we panic.

When I finally return home and move on with my life, there will be many questions I'll be asking myself. How do I deal with it? What do I do now? Can I still try to attain my original intended goal? The answers to these questions in order are, "Become resilient and brilliant.", "Keep moving forward.", and "Yes!".

I wasn't ready to become resilient on my journey. I didn't think I had the courage and strength to get through it. I anticipated at some point that I would give up. This anticipation didn't do me any good, and I continued to think pessimistically about my future. I always considered my time away in prison would be the toughest obstacle in my life. But my life is far from over.

Who knows if I will ever come across something much worse than what I experienced. I pray and hope that I never have to go through something else so traumatic to my life. The only way to secure this feat is to stay "resilient and brilliant", to avoid any future conflicts that could easily sabotage my life.

Will I run into problems as my life goes on? Yes. Do I want that? Absolutely. It's part of human nature and growth to learn how to overcome our problems, and we practice this task over and over while gaining resiliency. And where does the brilliance come into place?

Everyone is brilliant when it comes to knowing themselves. The only person who can know what's best for us is ourselves. We know how our awareness is going to help, how it's going to feel, and how it's going to benefit our lives. The feelings we take within and learn from ourselves is implemented, and we have an astute knowledge of how to live.

During my time away, it was challenging to try and learn through such an intense environment. I had distractions all around me, problems arising unexpectedly, and a new side of awareness for my senses to help me physically survive in such a dangerous facility. But if I wanted to continue living my life out, I had no choice but to learn from my experience to better myself mentally for my future.

I didn't have classes on it, nor did I have a tutor by my side for extra help. It was just me, and me alone. There was no curriculum planned out, and I had to each day improve myself to get to a state of resiliency. Sounds like a long process, doesn't it? Well, the process could take however long I needed it to be. There was no deadline for this project, just if I didn't end up a "deadline". And I mean that literally.

Today was a milestone in this journey. It was the end of it, the finale I've been waiting for six months. I felt like a new person, and that feeling will continue when I get home. I may always look the same in terms of my physical appearance, but my mental illness and internal feelings of emotions will change over time. And the best feeling for me, is accepting my emotions.

I tend to question myself regarding what needs to be done. It's good to surround yourself with questions, for the answers should embrace us with relief and satisfaction. It has come to me that the reason for my failures is the lack of confidence. The confidence I seek needs to be stronger than the desire to have it. What I need, is confidence to reach deep into my heart and mind. From there, the journey that's ahead of me can only be traveled willingly.

Having the will to continue living is the greatest power of all. But it's the control of the willpower that is the hardest responsibility. In fact, it's a challenge to take on. But willpower had nothing to do with gaining back willingness. The radical acceptance needed to be present, to understand why I needed to accept myself as an individual. And the same goes for anyone seeking radical acceptance in their life. All we can wait for are the results that will make or break us.

In recent years, I have focused on willfulness, the opposite of willingness. Willfulness is what I used to forget about fixing my life. I denied wanting to make it better, even when I knew the entire time that it was possible to change it. But I felt so comfortable sabotaging my life. For some reason, it felt good.

It was intended for others to feel sorry for me, trying to make them understand and be part of my suffering for them to help me. They weren't the answer to my all my problems. I was the answer. As I continued to deny my life, so did others. Why be a part of someone who wants nothing but negativity for themselves? The people in my life had no desire to share their willingness to help me. And for that, I was alone with my willfulness.

So, it was willingness that I required. I needed to be connected to the meaning of life. In this case, I needed to understand my own meaning of life. I do feel that the will to live is necessary to be a human being. Everyone has their own version of the meaning of their life. And it's simple to think about it this way.

One example is to be happy and embrace all your accomplishments. Another example could be to be surrounded by those who you truly love, and to be an asset in their lives. There is an endless amount of reasons as to why people choose willingness. I couldn't find my reason. But to find it, I needed to rid myself from all the willfulness I kept on seeking and pursuing.

It was willingness I needed to consume, like a drink to cleanse away the unwillingness I had on life. My participation in this world was waiting for me. The world was saying to me, "Join us. Be part of something wonderful, for only you can make it wonderful for yourself." Willingness began to glow inside of me, and I saw what the world had to offer.

Now I had to accept this great offer and take advantage of it. And so, I accepted the power of willingness. I remembered why I was still part of this world, and why I never succeeded in ending it. It's because I knew all along. I knew that I belonged here, and here I will stay.

After I packed all my belongings, and said my goodbyes, I moved out of the mental health unit. I arrived at the final exit of the facility, where I spent 20 minutes filling out paperwork, and another 20 minutes waiting with excitement and resiliency. I stood in front of the door that exited the county jail, as I waited for a knock on the door to then open, releasing me outside into the world I used to know. As I stood there, I thought about everything I went through these past six months. I also thought, what will the next six months bring me? The answer to that was all up to me, and only me.

And then it came. It all ended with a knock on the door.

Afterword

Quite a journey, isn't it? It's a journey I'll never forget. There may have been sections of it that will stick in your mind. And if that's the case, then this is a journey we have shared together.

Some people might define a journey as a vacation they took that left them with an unforgettable experience. Others might characterize it as a time that led them to a major accomplishment. Altogether, a journey will always have a beginning and an end, just like this book.

My journey wasn't a dream vacation that I've always wanted to go on. And it certainly wasn't an accomplishment I planned on achieving. It was a story of survival. What started as a nightmare, ended as an act of resiliency six months later. And it was when that word, "resiliency", and it's meaning, made me think differently about my life.

To this day, I still think about my time away and what occurred during this dark period of my life. I was arrested in my house and handcuffed to a bed for five days in an emergency room. I spent time incarcerated in a prison that offered me treatment. I made a close friend named Joe, who I will never forget. I fractured a bone for the first time in my life. I started a new year, as well as adding another year onto my age.

I was transferred to county jail, living in unbearable conditions. I saw a friend I made in jail kill himself. I appeared in court numerous times which depicted my future. I was released from my incarceration and came home feeling like a new person.

After reading this book, can you think of a time in your life when you felt resilient? I'm certain that in some point in your life, you have experienced it. And I'm certain that you will continue to feel resilient when the time comes again.

When that moment comes, be proud of it. Despite of what I went through, I'm still proud of myself. If there are unfortunate events in our lives that we choose to forget, don't forget them completely. In fact, it's normal to reminisce about these past events, so we can reflect on them to help us get through the present. These memories, these events, will never leave us. I know this journey, for me, will never be forgotten.

The odds that someone out there, in this world, dealing with major depression and suicidal ideations, has gone through such a similar journey as mine…are possible. Whether in the past, the present, or the future, the world is big enough for others like me to go through such a traumatic experience.

The way I see it now, and I encourage you to do the same, is that depression should not be ignored. As I wrote this book, I found that "there are many…" reasons why I came to this following conclusion:

There are many with depression. There are many who have attempted suicide, and many more who have succeeded at it. There are many affected by these suicides.

There are many who are receiving treatment for depression. There are many who have yet to reach out for help. There are many resources available to cope with depression, and many who are unaware of them.

There are many who do not understand the concept of depression. There are many scared of the topic "suicide". There are many who judge individuals with depression.

There are many with depression who believe there is hope. There are many who have become resilient during times of struggle and difficulty. There are many who cope with their depression successfully. There are many who are positive and optimistic about their future. There are many that have courage and strength to move on from their past.

There are many who have helped themselves and others who have depression.

I am one of them…and you can be too.

"Today you are you! That is truer than true! There is no one alive who is you-er than you!" – Dr. Seuss

www.ingramcontent.com/pod-product-compliance
Lightning Source LLC
Chambersburg PA
CBHW061753250726
48657CB00001B/108